Remembering Mississippi Freedom Summer

Charles O. Prickett

Remembering Mississippi Freedom Summer
© 2015 by Charles O. Prickett

ISBN: 978-1-941066-06-5

Library of Congress Control Number: 2015932046

Wordrunner Press
Petaluma, California

DEDICATION

This book is dedicated to all persons of color worldwide. In virtually every country there is discrimination practiced against anyone who looks different from the general population. But the most prevalent problem is discrimination against women, which has been going on for millions of years everywhere.

Contents

Remembering Mississippi
Freedom Summer

Introduction

I am Charles Prickett, raised as part of the white community in southern Illinois. Beginning at age eighteen, I was an active participant in the civil rights movement in the United States in the 1960s. This is my firsthand account of my experiences as a civil rights worker. Although I worked locally for equal rights in public accommodations in my hometown of Carbondale, Illinois, the main focus of this account is my involvement in nationwide events. These include the March on Washington (1963), the Mississippi Freedom Summer (1964), and the Selma-Montgomery March (1965).

Many photos in the book give the reader an actual image of the speaker and the other persons who are portrayed. A number of these are taken from a movie by Richard Beymer, "A Regular Bouquet." I have also used outtakes from the footage to illustrate the accounts of living in Mississippi in 1964 and the conditions that were prevalent during that time. Other photos were taken by me and others in Mississippi, Washington, D.C., and Selma, Alabama. Credit is given for the photos in the acknowledgements.

When lecturing on the civil rights movement to students and other interested groups, I am often asked how I got involved with the civil rights movement. The first reason is that my parents were always very supportive of equal rights for everyone. The second reason is that my sister Kay was very involved in the civil rights movement. She was the treasurer of the SIU chapter of the Student Nonviolent Coordinating Committee (SNCC). Third, our father always pointed out to us newspaper stories of the struggles of people of color for equal rights in our country. These three reasons contributed to my attitude about racial inequality and segregation that required personal action on my part to change the status quo.

Dad would clip out articles about the civil rights struggle from our various sources, including our local newspaper, the Southern Illinoisan, and make sure that Kay and I saw them. Then he would discuss them with us, and their implications for us and for our country. The most disturbing pictures were of people who were riding Greyhound and Trailways buses being beaten bloody with clubs as they tried to use the restrooms, waiting rooms, or lunch counters in cities across the South. Our mother was a reluctant supporter of civil rights, because she was a product of the Southern culture, and for her to take this stand in support of civil rights was a struggle.

Often, my grandparents and parents would meet Kay and me in the SIU cafeteria for coffee and snacks. At one such meeting, my sister and I were sitting at a neighboring table with friends. Some of our friends were black. My grandfather got up from his chair, opened his pocketknife, and approached our table. He looked around our table and announced, "You niggers stay away from my granddaughter." I got up from the table and told grandpa to put away his knife and led him to the table where he, my grandmother, and my parents were sitting. He calmed down a bit, and soon left the cafeteria. After that incident, our black friends seemed to have more respect for us because of the segregationist attitude toward race relations held by members of our family. They felt Kay and I were not only fighting those views in society, but within our own family as well.

When my sister and I worked in the civil rights movement in the South, our parents took out life insurance policies on both of us, so there would be enough money to bury us. Both of our parents felt that our chances of being murdered were very high.

In spite of their fears of losing their children, nevertheless they actually visited Kay and me at our projects in Mississippi. They were the only parents I saw visit their children in Mississippi during the summer of 1964. In retrospect, they were very brave and their fears were justified.

The civil rights movement was a unifying force for our entire country. My personal involvement in the civil rights movement has been a defining force in my life. Even though my work as a volunteer was an important factor in making our democratic system a reality for disenfranchised people, the real heroes are those who lived in the communities I was privileged to serve. The real tribute should be to those men, women, and children whose commitment to democratic ideals became a reality.

To me, the civil rights movement resulted in a triumph of democracy. For decades, black citizens were kept from voting because of restrictive voter registration laws. Due to the efforts made during the civil rights movement, black communities all over the South were organized and empowered, so much so that after the 1965 Voting Rights Act was passed, the result in Mississippi was more black elected public officials than any other state. That still rings true today.

I attended the March on Washington in 1963, participated as a volunteer and paid staff ($14 per week) in the Mississippi Freedom Summer of 1964, and helped organize and participated in the Selma-Montgomery March in 1965. This book chronicles these experiences, focusing on the local people from the black communities that were the crux of the civil rights movement. Each family has a story and these stories give insight into what it meant to be a member of the black community in the South in 1964. I became a member of that community.

This account begins with the March on Washington, a joyous gathering of people from every state and many countries who converged on Washington, D.C. in August of 1963. This event was totally peaceful and a celebration of the solidarity of most citizens of the United States on the issue of equal rights for all.

But when many of these same people converged on southern states, they encountered violent opposition that resulted in many beatings and death for anyone who sought to change the Jim Crow laws in these southern states.

A major portion of this book is concerned with the Mississippi Freedom Summer, and our work operating Freedom Schools, conducting voter registration drives, organizing the Mississippi Freedom Democratic Party (MFDP), and organizing local black farmers to vote in the Agricultural Stabilization Conservation Service (ASCS) fall elections. I was located in Madison County, Mississippi, Canton being the county seat.

Freedom Schools provided remedial education to children and adults who were prevented from attending the all white public schools by a section of the Mississippi Constitution. The all black schools operated only four months each school year so the children and their families could grow and pick cotton as sharecroppers for white landowners. The white schools were in session nine months each year. Freedom Schools helped to address this disparity of education which was imposed on the black community.

Registering to vote in Mississippi in 1964 was most often impossible if you were black. Black citizens had to pass a literacy test and pay poll taxes in order to register and vote. The literacy test used in Mississippi in 1964 is provided in Appendix III. Other examples from Louisiana and Alabama are also given. The purpose of these tests was to keep black citizens from registering to vote and voting. In spite of these barriers, black citizens tried again and again to register to vote. The 1965 Voting Rights Act stopped those practices.

The Mississippi Freedom Democratic Party (MFDP) was organized to give black citizens of Mississippi a voice in the political structure of Mississippi. The all white Mississippi Democratic Party (MDP) excluded people of color from membership, a reflection of the entire State of Mississippi, with its restrictive laws that prevented the registration of black voters. The Mississippi

Freedom Democratic Party (MFDP) challenged the credentials of the regular Mississippi Democratic Party (MDP) at the Democratic National Convention in Atlantic City, New Jersey in August of 1964. The Voting Rights Act was put in the public eye and was passed a year later by Congress because of the public sentiment garnered by the Mississippi Freedom Summer and the Mississippi Freedom Democratic Party.

The Agricultural Stabilization and Conservation Service (ASCS), an arm of the U.S. Department of Agriculture, held elections to local boards of farmers who administered federal farming subsidies. There had been no black farmers represented on these boards since their inception, even though sixty percent of the farm land in Madison County, Mississippi, was owned by black farmers. The election results changed this history, putting black representation on this board.

The events chronicled in Mississippi illustrate the apparent hatred for black citizens by the white majority, even though much of the economy of Mississippi was dependent upon the cheap labor provided by the black community. Exclusion of the black citizenry from the political process gave the black community a clear vision of the changes they wanted throughout the State of Mississippi and clearly helped those reforms become a reality. The push for local representation of black farmers on local boards became the main focus of our organizing efforts after the summer ended.

The Selma-Montgomery March typified the lack of respect afforded the U.S. Constitution across much of the South. The right to peaceful protest and to present political leaders with a list of grievances formed the legal basis for the federal court decision that ordered the State of Alabama to allow this march.

These momentous events changed the political, educational, economic, and social structures across the South. The effect has been a strengthening of our democratic form of government by the inclusion of many diverse voices in the political process.

1

The March on Washington

On a very hot day on August 28, 1963, I attended the March on Washington. There were hundreds of thousands of people gathered on the Capitol Mall between the Lincoln Memorial and the Washington Monument. The atmosphere was charged with a very positive outlook for the future of our nation and equality for all. People from every state in the union and many countries around the world convened on that hot summer day to celebrate what was then believed to be the beginning of the end to Jim Crow laws and racial prejudice around our great country. It seemed that everyone exuded enthusiasm and optimism for the future of civil rights for everyone in our country, regardless of the color of their skin.

I rode over twenty-four hours straight on a bus from Carbondale, Illinois to Washington, D.C. to be part of the historic march. There were not enough seats on the bus, so I lay in the aisle in a sleeping bag and slept as much as possible during that historic trip. When we arrived in Washington, we first went to one of the local churches for breakfast. It appeared that they had anticipated hundreds of thousands of people, as there was a seemingly inexhaustible supply of food. After being fed and warmly welcomed, we made our way to the Capitol Mall. There, we became part of the largest assembly of protestors this country had ever seen.

Attendees at the March on Washington cooling their feet in the reflecting pool between the Washington Monument and the Lincoln Memorial.

There was a solid mass of people from the Lincoln Memorial to the Washington Monument, and beyond. Everyone was in a great mood. It seemed like a family reunion, meeting long lost relatives. The charged atmosphere was one of love and support for everyone. I felt like I was among close friends and family as I wandered among the hundreds of thousands of people there to celebrate freedom for everyone. We were celebrating the realization that our Constitution indeed was our protector and applied to each and every one of us that day. The feeling of being connected and of solidarity was the strongest I have ever experienced in my life.

There were many speakers and entertainers. Pete Seeger, Peter, Paul and Mary, Joan Baez, Bob Dylan, Marian Anderson, and Mahalia Jackson all lent their voices to the cause. Even though we were entertained, the real entertainment was in the crowd itself. The joy of meeting people from around our country and the globe was the focus of everyone I met that day. I felt like everyone I met was a close friend, persons with whom I shared feelings of solidarity, love of country, and hope for the future. Even when the speakers began their diatribes against the status quo and Jim Crow, the crowd mainly stayed in the mode of relating person to person, not becoming engaged with the speakers or the presentations of the march organizers.

The next to last speaker was John Lewis, chairperson of Student Nonviolent Coordinating Committee (SNCC), the youngest speaker at the event. His speech, which a number of SNCC activists had helped write, took the Kennedy Administration to task for how little it had done to protect southern blacks and civil rights workers under attack in the Deep South. Cut from his original speech at the insistence of more conservative and pro-Kennedy leaders were phrases such as:

- "In good conscience, we cannot support wholeheartedly the administration's civil rights bill, for it is too little and too late. ..."

- "I want to know, which side is the federal government on?..."

- "The revolution is a serious one. Mr. Kennedy is trying to take the revolution out of the streets and put it into the courts. Listen, Mr. Kennedy. Listen, Mr. Congressman. Listen, fellow citizens. The black masses are on the march for jobs and freedom, and we must say to the politicians that there won't be a 'cooling off' period."

- "...We will march through the South, through the heart of Dixie, the way Sherman did. We shall pursue our own scorched earth policy and burn Jim Crow to the ground—nonviolently...."

These phrases do not seem extreme today. But in 1963, the country and the world were a much more conservative place. Any suggestion of confrontation was spurned; even the nonviolent kind that Lewis tried to support was jettisoned from his speech.

The last speaker was the Rev. Dr. Martin Luther King, Jr. When he began his speech, following John Lewis of SNCC, the crowd began to listen more attentively. Soon, "I Have A Dream"

Dr. King speaking at the March on Washington

was in everyone's mind. Dr. King's famous speech is in Appendix I. The entire assembly stopped speaking to each other, stopped milling around, and started listening closely. King began by signifying this 100 year anniversary of the Emancipation Proclamation, "Five score years ago, a great American, in whose symbolic shadow we stand, signed the Emancipation Proclamation. This momentous decree came as a great beacon light of hope to millions of Negro slaves who had been seared in the flames of withering injustice. It came as a joyous daybreak to end the long night of captivity." King's words, "I have a dream that my four children will one day live in a nation where one day they will not be judged by the color of their skin but by the content of their character" resonated with everyone that day. His words hit a chord with the hearts and minds of the entire assembly. Rev. King's speech was a show stopper, and everyone stood still and listened to him put into words what we all felt in our hearts.

That day marked the beginning of public awareness of the problems associated with racial prejudice in our country. As the public became aware of citizens being denied the right to vote, the right to peacefully assemble, to engage in freedom of speech, all based upon the color of their skin, public opinion changed, as did political support for the civil rights movement.

It would be nearly a year later when the first of two land-mark pieces of legislation were passed. The first is the 1964 Civil Rights Act, and the second is the 1965 Voting Rights Act. Both changed the economic, political, educational, and social structure of our country. These Acts paved the road we are still traveling to realize "the Dream" fulfilled, the Dream that Rev. Dr. Martin Luther King, Jr. spoke of on that hot day in Washington, D.C.

Dr. King's speech and the news media coverage was the glim-mer of hope that became a beacon of light that shone its way into the hearts and minds of all Americans. This day marked a distinct turning point in the struggle for equal rights for all in our diverse country. This day awakened the sensitivity of America to the sordid plight of perceived second class citizens who, because of the color of their skin, were being relegated to poverty, poor living conditions, substandard public education, a lack of access to public accommodations, and a lack of health care. These people of color had sacrificed their lives for the good of their county since the Revolutionary War. Now, their voices would be heard. Their children would no longer be seen wearing rags for clothes and no shoes. Their education in our nations public schools would be shown to be segregated, in violation of the U.S. Supreme Court nine years earlier. After the March on Washington, people of color would be seen and heard. The change would take years but the momentum for change would continue to gain energy. On this day, many realized that chang-es were indeed coming.

2

Mississippi Freedom Summer

Nineteen sixty-four was a turbulent year in America and calls for revolution in the racist societies of the South were heard everywhere. The battleground was the State of Mississippi. Battles raged over voting rights, the right to register to vote, the right to peaceably assemble, the right to run for and hold public office, and the right to attend public schools. At first glance, all these rights are embedded in the U.S. Constitution as the Bill of Rights. But one thing was made very clear: They were not recognized for black citizens in Mississippi in 1964.

I was in this revolution, and was part of the civil rights movement in the 1960s across the South. Many people participated in the civil rights movement, including my sister, and many of our friends. Some of us may have had an idea of what we were getting into. But I, for one, really had no clear idea of what it would be like working in the South for civil rights.

I found out that Mississippi was a dangerous place for anyone viewed as an outsider, not a native Mississipian. I found that the black population of Mississippi was widely discriminated against in all aspects of society, including commerce, education, politics, and social activities. But I also found that the black citizens of Mississippi were willing to do what was necessary to end this scourge of discrimination by standing up to the white power structure and by putting themselves and their families at risk.

The Mississippi Freedom Summer had specific goals which I pursued during my engagement in the civil rights movement in Mississippi. The goals were articulated and organized by the Student Nonviolent Coordinating Committee (SNCC) and the Congress of Racial Equality (CORE), under the umbrella organization of the Council of Federated Organizations (COFO). The State of Mississippi was divided up into projects in almost every county. Each county had a project director who coordinated the activities of the volunteers who helped pursue the goals.

These four goals were:

- Freedom Schools: Remedial education for children and adults was offered at most projects across the state.

- Voter Registration: Challenge the State of Mississippi voter registration laws, including literacy tests and poll taxes.

- The Mississippi Freedom Democratic Party: The Mississippi Freedom Democratic Party (MFDP) was organized statewide to give black citizens a platform to challenge candidates in local and statewide elections as well as seeking recognition at the Democratic National Convention held in Atlantic City, New Jersey, in 1964.

- Empowering Farmers: The U.S. Department of Agriculture held elections in each county for representatives to the Agricultural Stabilization and Conservation Service (ASCS), which administered federal programs to farmers. In the fall of 1964, the first black representatives ran for this board and were elected. The push for black representation on these boards was not part of our activities during the summer, but became our main focus in the fall of 1964.

A: Nonviolent Training: Key to Survival

Early in the summer of 1964, I was in New York working at the Student Nonviolent Coordinating Committee (SNCC) office fund-raising for the civil rights movement. When a call came in for more civil rights workers for the Mississippi Freedom Summer, I quickly volunteered. In just a few days, I was on my way to Mississippi. I felt nothing but disdain for those who were deny-ing basic rights to people of color and I wanted to treat them like they treated those who they beat with baseball bats and axe handles. I wanted to beat them so they would understand what it felt like. But the nonviolent training I received changed my attitude.

Before my departure, the church I was attending, Antioch Baptist Church in Brooklyn, showed its support. Through their pastor, Rev. George Lawrence, they donated five hundred dollars to the Student Nonviolent Coordinating Committee (SNCC). Rev. Lawrence had attended the March on Washington the previous summer, as I had, and we shared this powerful experience. He was a very down-to-earth man with great compassion for every-one. He was an inspiration from the pulpit and for civil rights in our country and specifically the Bedford-Stuyvesant neighbor-hood in Brooklyn where the church is located.

My trip to Mississippi began in New York. I drove a car that was donated to Student Nonviolent Coordinating Committee (SNCC) from New York to Washington, D.C., where we would receive mandatory nonviolence training. There were three of us in that 1960 Ford and we were all quite young, in our late teens or early twenties. We were an integrated group, all civil rights workers, and we talked continuously about our position as people in the changing racial climate in the United States, and in the South.

Jimmy was a tall, thin eighteen year old with a warm smile and a steely determination. He felt a personal responsibility to help make life a better place for the millions of disenfranchised blacks in the South. He felt personally impacted by all that had happened to the black communities in the South. His youth and naiveté were readily apparent, but he was not to be deterred. Jimmy called his mother every afternoon around 5: 00 p.m., as he had to make that promise to her for permission to go south. The day we all left for Washington D.C., she held him close and cried, but wished us well. She, too, felt she was a part of what we were doing, as she sent her baby boy into the conflict, not knowing if she would ever see him again.

Our other companion, George, was a very quiet person who did not say much. When he did speak, it was well thought out and supported with references to literature and statistics. George was in his first year of college, but felt that he wanted to actualize his philosophy of social change by confronting the ills of society. He was not satisfied with reading about conflict and resolution, but wanted actual experience with real people in real situations in the process of identifying, strategizing, and changing basic issues associated with citizenship that were unequally distributed based upon race and poverty. George's quiet contemplation kept us grounded and helped us articulate our shared reasons for involvement in the civil rights movement. He seemed so logical and articulate, that we often deferred to his reasoning as to why we were on this journey.

Our discussions over the next two weeks probed the depths of our personal commitment to this crusade for freedom. We felt that our own sense of personal and collective freedom of expression to be an active player in our democratic form of government depended upon the realization of these same rights and freedoms for all citizens of the United States. If anyone remained shackled by Jim Crow laws, which prevented the exercise of those rights, then all of us were also prevented from the free exercise of those same rights. And, ironically, none of us were old enough to register to vote, as the voting age then was twenty-one!

We were cognizant that we could die at the hands of the segregationists who had killed numerous civil rights workers over the years. Even though we were young, we did not feel like we would live forever. We recognized and embraced the fact that we might never return to our families and friends. This feeling did not engender fear and trepidation in us, but made us feel empowered, because we felt part of a philosophy and social movement that was larger and more important than we were as individuals. However, our conversations and discussions did not center on that topic. We felt we were helping right a long history of injustice toward United States citizens who happened to be black. We felt like we were preparing for a war, as we were eager to join the other volunteers already in Mississippi.

We stayed in Washington for about a week, receiving nonviolent training. We stayed at the apartment of Topper Carew, a young architect. He opened his home to three strangers, shared his food, shelter, and support with us, and made us feel completely welcome in his home. He was not going to Mississippi himself as part of the Mississippi Freedom Summer, but he was adamant about enabling civil rights for everyone by designing living and working spaces that encouraged everyone to work and live together. Mr. Carew eventually became a filmmaker and screenwriter. One of his productions is "D.C. Cab" starring Mr. T.

The nonviolent training we received was very serious and centered upon the kind of philosophy modeled by Gandhi, who brought the British Empire to its knees in India. We could not use violence even though the white opposition was fully armed and dedicated to using whatever means they thought they needed to rid their state of us, those "outside agitators." For me, this was a change in the way I acted and thought. My primary motivation in getting involved in civil rights was centered upon my horror at seeing pictures of other civil rights workers beaten just because they had a different color of skin, or they acted in a way that was interpreted as a threat to the white power structure.

The behavior that was interpreted by the white citizenry as threats were, in my view, not a credible threat to the racist status quo. Acts such as going to the white bathroom, using the white drinking fountain, or using the white waiting room were not revolutionary activities. I wanted to beat those white thugs just as they had beaten those who they perceived as a threat to segregation. I saw their actions and attitudes as an excuse to engage in violence towards others, not as a reaction to a perceived threat to racial segregation. My attitude had to change if I were to survive, and it did change, when I incorporated into my behavior the training for reacting to violence in a nonviolent manner. But my behavior reverted back on one occasion when I encountered the Madison County Sheriff and his deputies in Madison County, Mississippi, later that summer.

We were taught to roll up in a ball and protect our midsection from kicking and beating. We were taught to keep our thoughts to ourselves, as any verbal outburst of defiance would surely give a white person justification to injure or kill us. One anecdote that is still fresh in my mind was hearing that at least one civil rights worker asked to pray before the white racists began

Nonviolent training: roll up into a ball and protect yourself.

to beat him. As he began to speak to God, he also spoke to the white racists by asking God to forgive them and citing scriptures that supported forgiveness and loving thy neighbor as thyself. In that instance, the civil rights worker escaped with no injuries, as the heat of the moment subsided. We were encouraged to continue speaking as long as possible with the hope that the energy that was being focused upon we who were about to be beaten would in turn focus on those about to beat us, our fellow man.

We were told that we would probably be beaten, and maybe killed. Everyone was given a chance to opt out of going to Mississippi. No one refused to go, but it was a close call for some. The training did not prepare us for when we encountered law enforcement personnel and other white people in Mississippi. In Mississippi, reality set in, as we learned to react in a way that would keep us from being killed or beaten. We were trained to speak to the individual person or persons who was threatening us and try to have him or her see us as a person, not a symbol or threat to their way of life. The philosophy of the nonviolent training was "an exercise in passion," as explained by my sister Kay, who was also a civil rights worker and attended her training in Oxford, Ohio.

Kay stated, "The best thinkers in the nation engaged our minds and the charismatic veterans taught us how to sing. Everyone there had definite ideas and strong personalities and the atmosphere was electric. For the first time in my life, I was in a situation for which there was no pre-prescribed solution. Creativity, deep thinking and adjustment to a new culture were required. We were totally engaged and we saw that we could make a difference. During the second week of training, news came that Michael Schwerner, James Chaney, and Andrew Goodman were missing. Rita Schwerner, Michael's wife, was there and the veterans did not say what they were almost certain of: That the three were dead. Singing carried us through that week and through the whole summer. We held each other and sang. We were one. We were invincible."

On at least one occasion, I used the fact that my father was a Mason to try and change the direction of what seemed an inevitable physical encounter with the local sheriff. I noticed a Masonic ring on the finger of the Sheriff of Madison County, and began a conversation about his local Masonic Lodge and the one my father belonged to. I saw him pause in his aggression toward me and his usual condemnation of our activities, and he seemed to have second thoughts after learning my father was a Mason like him. Actually, he liked to arrest (detain) us and then let us go after a time of physical abuse and individual harassment.

Encounters with the local sheriff taught me how important it was to establish some kind of link or shared attribute with those who were wanting to cause me harm. There were other instances as well, but not all were successful. Local whites did not want to talk to me or recognize some shared experience or belief. But on the rare occasions when we did actually communicate, the threat of violence abated. This was probably the most important lesson and strategy I learned during our nonviolent training.

My sister Kay offered additional insights into confronting the dangers of going to Mississippi: "Our trainers emphasized that no one should feel badly about going home. There was a good chance that we would be shot the minute we stepped off the bus in Mississippi. Danger would be constant. I considered these arguments and came to terms with my own death. I realized that backing down to save one's own skin when the right and necessary action was clear was tantamount to death. If death came, it would come while I was truly alive and (as McLuhan said) living life mythically and in depth. Life was in the direction of creative action. I chose life."

After receiving nonviolent training, we continued in the Ford to Atlanta. As we rolled into the Deep South, we were struck by the not so subtle changes in social norms. As we got further and further into the South, we could not find restaurants that would serve all of us. We began to see and feel the oppression of segregation in America. We began to realize that our fears of being the focus of violent acts against us because of our race was very real. The transition from New York to Washington, D.C. and points south was gradual, but the effect on all of us was evident. We began watching cars we thought were following us. We watched people in restaurants look at us because we were an integrated group. We felt the sting of racial prejudice in the stares of people on the road. And we were denied services because we were a racially diverse group.

Atlanta was a center of organizations dedicated to the civil rights struggle. It seemed that no one slept at the Student Nonviolent Coordinating Committee (SNCC) offices, as I was there for a day or two and the office was always active, day and night. This was the nerve center for the national civil rights movement, and was a very exciting place to be. But it was also in the South, and when I ventured away from the offices, it was clearly an environment that was not friendly or supportive to civil rights, but violent and dangerous. Even though I liked this electrifying atmosphere, I had to go to Mississippi. I finally booked a flight from Atlanta to Jackson, Mississippi.

Upon my arrival in Jackson, I was met at the airport by Student Nonviolent Coordinating Committee (SNCC) volunteers. The air was thick and heavy in Jackson that hot and humid morning but in spite of all that had occurred in recent months, the attitude of the Student Nonviolent Coordinating Committee (SNCC) volunteers was very positive. No one seemed to be thinking about the murder of Medgar Evers (assassinated June 12, 1963, in Jackson, Mississippi) or the possibility of us being ambushed and killed. I was taken to the Council of Federated Organizations (COFO) office on Lynch Street in Jackson. The street name seemed ironic for the location of the main civil rights office in Mississippi. What I was not prepared for was the level of hate we encountered from the white community. The majority of white people I encountered seemed afraid of the social, economic, political, and educational changes which we were trying to accomplish through our efforts in the black community.

Why did the white community in Mississippi hate us so? I knew, of course, that simply being associated with the civil rights movement in the South was reason enough. But what was driving that unbridled hate? I concluded it was fear. Fear of the changes we were trying to make in education, politics, economics, and society in general. Fear that if children of all colors were to be educated together, white racial purity would be lost. Fear that if a living wage were to be paid to sharecroppers, the agrarian economic system would collapse because of high labor costs. Fear that if blacks got the right to vote, they would take over the government and exact reprisals from the white power structure that had taken advantage of the uneducated, economically depressed, and politically impotent black community for centuries.

The thinking that led to violence and murder against civil rights workers was ingrained in the culture and psyche of the South. White Southerners felt justified in their hate for anyone who articulated support for people of color. These same Southerners, most of whom considered themselves Christians and attended church regularly, chose to hate those persons whom they viewed as a threat. This hatred, the deaths of the three civil rights workers, and the injustice that occurred can be illustrated in the excerpts taken from the declaration of Horace D. Barnette, who participated in the murders of James Chaney, Andrew Goodman, and Michael Schwerner. The full declaration of Horace D. Barnette is in Appendix II. The mindset of the murderers show how little they valued human life when the victims were black, or took a position that was at odds with their racist attitudes.

Mr. Barnette's declaration is dated November 2, 1964. It is witnessed by two FBI agents. Mr. Barnette describes going to Akins Trailer Park in Meridian, Mississippi, to do a job for the Klan on June 21, 1964. He says he "did not know what the job

This poster of the three murdered civil rights workers was posted in nearly every black home in the summer of 1964.

was." When he arrived at the trailer park, he was met by Preacher Killen and several others. Killen told him that three civil rights workers had been released from jail and that "we were going to catch them and give them a whipping." After meeting with Barnette and other men in Philadelphia, Mississippi, Killen said "we have a place to bury them, and a man to run the dozer to cover them up."

The car in which the three civil rights workers were riding was stopped by Neshoba County Deputy Sheriff Price on a side road near Philadelphia, Mississippi. Barnette said that Price "told them to get out and get into his car. Price took his blackjack and struck Chaney on the back of the head. The men drove a few miles and then Deputy Price and the other men turned off Highway 19 on a gravel road and stopped. One of the men drove the 1963 Ford in which the three civil rights workers had been riding. Wayne, one of the men in the group, ran up to Price's car, opened the left rear door, pulled Schwerner out of the car, spun him around so that Schwerner was standing on the left side of the road, with his back to the ditch and said, 'Are you that nigger lover?' and Schwerner said, 'Sir, I know just how you feel.' Wayne had a pistol in his right hand, then shot Schwerner. Wayne then went back to Price's car and got Goodman, took him to the left side of the road with Goodman facing the road, and shot Goodman. At this time Jim Jordan said 'Save one for me.' He then got out of Price's car and got Chaney out. After he shot Chaney, Jordan then said 'You didn't leave me anything but a nigger, but at least I killed me a nigger.'"

The burned car they were driving was found on June 23, 1964. The bodies of these murdered civil rights workers were found on August 4, 1964. The State of Mississippi refused to prosecute the murders, citing a lack of evidence.

On December 4, 1964, the suspects were charged in U.S. Federal District Court in Jackson, Mississippi, for interfering with the civil rights of the murdered men. After lengthy appeals, including the U.S. Supreme Court, the trial court convicted seven of the murderers and acquitted nine. This was October 27, 1967. None of the murderers spent more than six years in jail.

Reverend (Preacher) Killen was free from prosecution until 2004, forty years after his participation in these grisly murders. Even after his conviction for manslaughter, he was not imprisoned, because his attorneys had filed an appeal and the judge freed him without bail pending the outcome of the appeal. It took public protests and pressure by the news media to force a trial. It took more pressure to finally incarcerate Reverend Killen during the appeal process. But the thinking that led to these three murders in 1964 persisted into the next millennia.

B: Arriving in Mississippi

My first impression of the Council of Federated Organizations (COFO) office on Lynch St. was that no one was in charge, and everyone was there to caution me and tell me what was expected of a new volunteer. Some people just sat around discussing different strategies for challenging the "white power structure," as it was called. Others were talking on the telephone. There were WATS (wide area telephone service) lines on which a telephone call could be made without incurring long distance charges. Since many of the people were out of state, there was a long wait to get to use a WATS line. A few people were typing reports and letters but most were simply there talking, sitting, drinking coffee, and visiting. It was a pretty relaxed atmosphere amid the reports of beatings, murders, and violence that became a part of my daily life as my tenure as a civil rights volunteer continued into the fall.

Charles in the COFO offices on Lynch St. in Jackson, Mississippi, in 1964.

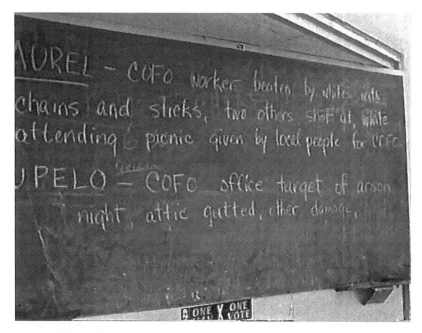

Blackboard in the COFO office telling of beatings and arson in Laurel and Tupelo Mississippi. The targets were COFO workers and offices.

The COFO office on Lynch St. in Jackson in 1964.

The Mississippi Freedom Summer was an attempt to address four issues which plagued the black communities throughout Mississippi. A common goal of all four issues was to establish local leadership to extend these efforts beyond the summer.

First were Freedom Schools. Black schools in Mississippi were segregated, even though this was ten years after the U.S. Supreme Court's unanimous decision declaring segregated schools "inherently unequal" in *Brown vs. Board of Education*. Black schools were in session four months each year while white students attended school for nine months. We held classes on basic skills for black children. What we did not anticipate was the attendance of the parents of these children. Adult literacy was soon added to our curriculum. Freedom Schools directly addressed the unequal and segregated public schools in Mississippi, and the poor education received by black children and their parents. Freedom Schools were designed to meet the needs of the local communities, providing remedial instruction in math, reading, and writing. Topics such as black history and current events provided an opportunity to openly discuss issues that were pivotal to the success and future of the black communities.

Second was voter registration. It was virtually impossible for a black person to register to vote in 1964, but it was a badge of honor to keep trying, in spite of literacy tests that were impossible to pass. A year later, Congress passed the Voting Rights Act which outlawed literacy tests, poll taxes, and made it possible for black citizens to finally register and vote. Today, there are more black elected officials in Mississippi than any other state.

Third was the Mississippi Freedom Democratic Party (MFDP). The all white Mississippi Democratic Party (MDP) did not support the party platform of the National Democratic Party nor their presidential nominee, Lyndon Johnson. The Mississippi Freedom Democratic Party (MFDP) held meetings state wide and elected delegates to the Democratic National Convention held in Atlantic City, New Jersey. The Mississippi Freedom Democratic Party delegates challenged the credentials of the

A volunteer speaks to a man about registering to vote.

Mississippi Democratic Party, but failed to get seated at the convention. Fannie Lou Hamer, an outspoken Mississippi Freedom Democratic Party delegate, opened the eyes of America to the plight of black citizens throughout the South with her nationally televised heartfelt testimony before the credentials committee.

Fourth was organizing black farmers for the election to the local board of the U.S. Department of Agriculture Agricultural Stabilization and Conservation Service (ASCS). The Agriculture Agricultural Stabilization and Conservation Service (ASCS) is an arm of the U.S. Department of Agriculture. A locally elected board determines which farmers get acreage allotments for crops and the myriad of subsidies given to farmers. Madison County black farmers owned sixty percent of the land but had never been represented on the local board. We organized black farmers to vote for a slate of candidates for the board of the Agriculture Agricultural Stabilization and Conservation Service (ASCS). Elections were to be held in the fall in about three months. The restrictive voter registration laws of the State of Mississippi did not apply to these elections, as they were solely run by the U.S. Department of Agriculture. In 1964, the first black farmers were elected to this board.

The days of the volunteers were filled with activities which addressed the four goals they came to Mississippi to accomplish. There was little time to do the things that needed to be done simply in order to live in some degree of comfort. The volunteers spent long hours preparing for and teaching Freedom School, working on voter registration campaigns, organizing the Mississippi Freedom Democratic Party (MFDP), and organizing black farmers to challenge the candidates for representation on the local boards that doled out federal subsidies for farmers.

In the summer, most of our work was teaching Freedom School. We prepared plans for various lessons, games for the children, and stories for everyone who attended Freedom School at a local church. We offered classes in math and reading, and some college preparatory classes for the high school students who had never before dreamed of attending college. We tried to make the children and their parents realize that they could benefit from an education and the children could go to college.

Life skills, when viewed through the eyes of some of the adults in the black community, rarely included academic skills. Activities such as growing vegetables, tending chickens, and dressing game were much more relevant to survival than reading a newspaper. No one I knew in Madison County even subscribed to a newspaper, except George Washington in Canton, who sold them in his store. Since everyone around Valley View was involved in agriculture, skills such as knowing how to put harness on a mule and plow a field, were basic and necessary. Among children, knowing how to pick cotton and tend the family garden were part of their necessary skill set. But, it was easy to convince local families that they needed academic skills, even when such skills were not necessary for survival.

Organizing was a difficult task, as the local people worked all day just to support themselves and their families. The best we could do was to get them to attend a meeting in the evening at a local church. These meetings were focused on organizing efforts aimed at registering to vote, and organizing the local farmers to vote in the fall elections for the U.S. Department of Agriculture Agricultural Stabilization and Conservation Service (ASCS) board. Because nearly everyone in the Valley View area was involved with agriculture, meetings were well attended and interest was high. The prospect of improving economic conditions was an attractive concept for families struggling to find money for food, clothing, transportation, and basic necessities of life.

Getting people to try and register to vote was fraught with danger, mostly to them. Nearly everyone had families who were subject to reprisals if even one member of the family tried to register to vote. It should have been difficult to convince someone to go to the courthouse and stand in line for hours, fill out a lengthy form, be the target of insults, take the literacy test, have your name published in the paper, and suffer the consequences. For example, when the applicant indicated their employer on the form, many were fired by the time they returned home. Further, few people were found qualified to vote, so the entire process and the consequences were without any payoff. But, in spite of all these negative effects, many people continued to try and register to vote, for which they paid a price. They looked with pride on their attempts to become registered voters and be a part of the democratic process. They wanted a voice in their government.

The Civil Rights Act of 1964, enacted July 2, 1964, was landmark legislation in the United States that outlawed major forms of racial discrimination against black citizens and against women. Its purpose was to end racial segregation in the workplace and in facilities that served the general public. The preamble to this legislation begins with, "To enforce the constitutional right to vote, ..." This important legislation had no effect on voting in Mississippi or anywhere else when it was passed. This legislation had a narrow focus, that of addressing discrimination in public accommodations, in hiring and on the job, with the establishment of the Equal Employment Opportunity Commission (EEOC). It was completely ignored throughout the South, just as was the unanimous Supreme Court decision in *Brown vs. Board of Education*.

The following year, The Voting Rights Act of 1965 was passed. It is another landmark piece of legislation in the United States that outlawed discriminatory voting practices that had been responsible for the widespread disenfranchisement of black citizens for decades. Echoing the language of the Fifteenth Amendment, the Act prohibits states from imposing any "voting qualification or prerequisite to voting, or standard, practice, or procedure ... to deny or abridge the right of any citizen of the United States to vote on account of race or color." Specifically, Congress intended the Act to outlaw the practice of requiring otherwise qualified voters to pass literacy tests in order to register to vote, as well as paying a poll tax in order to vote, principal means by which Southern states had prevented black citizens from exercising their right to vote. This law did have an effect on voting rights in Mississippi, because its implementation included federal examiners to monitor the registration of black voters and prevented the local registrars from continuing their discriminatory practices.

C: Life in Valley View: Summer

Canton, Mississippi, was my first stop at a civil rights project. I met George Raymond, the no nonsense director of the civil rights projects in Madison County, Mississippi. George, who was from New Orleans, was a Freedom Rider in 1961, and participated in the sit-ins at the Woolworth lunch counter in Jackson, Mississippi, in 1963. He influenced his mother and his family to get involved in the civil rights movement.

George was clearly in charge and seemed somewhat perturbed at having yet another volunteer for whom he was responsible. I think he was overwhelmed with responsibilities, including creating and carrying out strategies for registering black citizens to vote, being sure that Freedom Schools were operating throughout the county, organizing black farmers to vote in Agricultural Stabilization Conservation Service (ASCS) elections in the fall, and organizing the Mississippi Freedom Democratic Party. George sent me to Valley View, which was in need of more volunteers, particularly as Freedom School teachers.

Valley View was the northernmost project in Madison County. It was deemed "somewhat safe" because of the strong solidarity among the black farmers who lived and worked there. Valley View was a small loosely knit community of farmers who looked out for one another, but had very little organization socially, except for attendance at church and use of the cooperative cotton gin. And even the religious aspect of this rural society was somewhat fractured, as people attended different churches, depending upon who was preaching, or if there was someone they wanted to see in a neighboring area.

When I arrived at Valley View, I was met by the other volunteers, both black and white. At least six volunteers lived in the Freedom House, a small two bedroom structure near the intersection of three country roads. One road was oil and chip, one gravel, and the other was dirt (really mostly sand). Right at this intersection, there was a small country store, about

Phil walking near the Freedom House. The store is the structure shown and the shower is to the right of the store.

300 square feet of space. The store had one room and wooden shelves around the walls. Everything was crammed into these shelves, including most household goods, canned goods, motor oil, bread, candy, and detergent. The proprietor and owner, Mr. Williams, was very accommodating and helpful. He would get you nearly anything you wanted as long as you were willing to wait a few days. He also cashed the checks for the volunteers.

I lived in the two bedroom, one bath Freedom House with several other volunteers. Saying it was a one bath house is an understatement. We had no use of the toilet, sink, or tub because there was no running water in the house. The nearest water was from a well in our front yard. The front yard was dirt and became mud when it rained.

I was shown some places to sleep in the Freedom House, and chose a couch, but there was no guarantee that it would be available when it came time for sleep. Sleeping arrangements were haphazard. I found out that the schedules of all the volunteers were as varied as their personalities. From the beginning, it seemed like there was no organized method of living in this small house. Eating seemed to be one's own responsibility, in spite of the fact that many people seemed to depend upon whatever food was available. Food was in short supply, so we were encouraged to get money from our friends and families from the North in order to feed the volunteers on the project. The Freedom House served as the base of our operations. Of the two bedrooms, one was an office, and the other was used for sleeping.

It is an understatement to say that the Valley View Freedom House was crowded. Everyone was very cooperative and overcrowding did not seem to be an issue with anyone. The real issue however was food. We had very little food, and no one cooked for the entire group. Because we were living in a rural area, most of the neighbors had their own gardens. They shared their produce with us in the Freedom House. We had a lot of greens that summer, as well as beans, tomatoes, and zucchini. I don't know what we would have done without the support of the local community.

The volunteers with whom I shared this small refuge were from all over the U.S. John was from Boston and was a public school teacher. John was so patient with all of his students that his effectiveness as a teacher was amplified. Students gravitated to him because he always spent extra time one-on-one with students with special problems with language. He was also responsible for making lists of new words which the students snapped up. It was his lists which became so popular with the students and their families. New words traveled quickly in our small community. They were discussed and incorporated into writing and speech by our students and their families. After handing out a list of words, we would hear them the next day, or read them in the essays and other writings of the students.

John was also a dedicated runner. Most mornings he trained for the Boston Marathon by running the dusty county roads for a few hours before we left for Freedom School. Although he was repeatedly warned about any encounter with local white people, he persisted in his training. He made many contributions to our project, including the publication of the "Pleasant Green Magazine," a collection of essays, poems and articles written by our students.

Phil, a volunteer from New York, was a teacher in a private school before coming to Mississippi. He was in tune with the local students and the community. He became a part of the local community just by his sensitivity and warm nature. Phil's students were all special to him. Like John, he spent extra time with students who needed individualized instruction. Phil also organized group activities such as line dancing and circle games where a student was inside the circle and chose another student to answer a question so he or she could get out of the middle and into the circle.

Another volunteer was Bill who had a Jeep which was purchased by his grandmother to use in Mississippi. He was enormously

A copy of the "Pleasant Green Magazine," August 1964.

Phil organizing a group activity at Freedom School.

affected by the people he encountered and realized how much work remained to be done in Madison County, so he left for a brief trip up North to get permission to take a year off from college and, incidentally, to persuade his family that he really needed a Jeep to get around the slippery roads of Mississippi when it rained. They agreed, thinking that after his return they would be able to use the Jeep on the family farm in Connecticut. So, in September, after the end of the formal Freedom Summer projects, and after many of the volunteers had left to return to school, he appeared with his Jeep covered with stickers proclaiming support for the civil rights movement, mostly, "We Shall Overcome: SNCC" stickers.

When it came time for the scheduled service on this new vehicle, the local dealer refused to service it because it was being used in the civil rights movement. It wasn't until the intervention by Bill's father that the local dealership relented and serviced the vehicle. Then it took months before they returned it. At the end of the summer, Bill continued to work as a Congress of Racial Equality (CORE) staff member through the following year. He made $14 per week. Bill's commitment typified that of all the volunteers, most of whom maintained contact with their friends living in and around Valley View.

Rodney, another volunteer from New York, was skinny and nervous. He couldn't sleep at night for fear that we would be attacked, killed, or the house would be burned. He kept lookout a great deal of the time. He was a welcome companion during our watch assignments, as he was a great conversationalist and philosopher. He could talk at length on nearly any subject, and did. He was also a gifted teacher, being able to reach students with the least amount of skills. He taught these students how to read and decipher the intricacies of the English language, both oral and written. He was also an excellent sounding board for any ideas anyone had for reaching out to the local community and spurring those ideas into action. I always felt safer when Rodney was on watch.

One of the first people I met at the Valley View project was Richard Beymer who was a well-known movie star at that time.

Rodney, a great companion and philosopher.

He had starred in "West Side Story" as Tony, opposite Natalie Wood. He was tall, good looking, and famous. He had driven his Austin Healy 3000 to Mississippi from California. It still bore California license plates, which were seen by some as a public challenge to the white racists. Almost every one of the volunteers who had a car registered it in Mississippi and received Mississippi license plates. That way, it appeared that you might be from Mississippi, and it attracted less attention. The vehicle registration clerks were always happy to take our money for the registration and new license plates. Richard declined this process.

Richard decided to film scenes from our Freedom School and voter registration drives. I worked with him on this project around the state filming what civil rights projects were doing and highlighting the effects on the local communities. We visited various projects around the state, filming mass meetings, voter registration drives, and Freedom Schools. We also interviewed many local people who were involved in the civil rights struggle. Richard produced the movie, "A Regular Bouquet," in 1964, which has been shown nationwide since that time.

Richard also was very generous in supporting the Valley View project. He spent over $200 per week on groceries and other items to support the project. He even took us to a local country store that sold beer and had a jukebox. We danced and drank quarts of beer a few times. We rarely ventured out at night, unless we were attending a meeting. These were really times to let our hair down and have some fun, something we all missed. Even though Richard was a Hollywood star, he remained down to Earth and true to his Iowa roots.

During our rare trips to town, we were often stopped by the local police or sheriff and asked for identification. The local law enforcement agencies asked all civil rights workers to register with them, supposedly so they could help protect us. But as they were members of the Klan and/or White Citizens Council themselves, all it did was to give them information about us that they could use to intimidate and harass us and our friends and families. I always refused to cooperate, but several other volunteers showed their local registration as a civil rights worker to the police when asked. I would not register, as I considered myself to be a citizen of the United States, and had the right to be anywhere in our country. Upon refusal to identify myself, the officer always walked away. I always wondered who would protect us from them, as they were the very people who were harassing and arresting us for trumped up violations of the law. They were also those responsible for church burnings and murders that summer and for decades before.

Andrew Lee Green, or Andy or Green, was our project director. Andy had come south from St. Louis to become a part of the civil rights movement. He met and fell in love with a local woman, Lil Bit. She got that name soon after her birth because she was a very tiny baby. The name stuck, but she was far from tiny as an adult. Andy moved in with her and her family and became part of the local community. Andy drove one of the cars assigned to our project to and from his adopted home.

Around the end of the summer, it became apparent that Andy could neither read nor write, and did not possess a driver's license. He could no longer drive because liability insurance did not cover unlicensed drivers. Andy was too self conscious and ashamed to admit his lack of communication skills. But when confronted, he admitted he could not read and write. The volunteers rallied to help Andy. In a few weeks, with one-on-one tutorials from the Freedom School teachers, Andy made remarkable progress. His written communication skills improved to the point that he tackled the driver's license examination in Mississippi and passed on his first attempt.

Andy was enthusiastic and had a very positive outlook for the success of the entire civil rights movement. But he lacked a plan to put into action the goals of the movement. He didn't know how to register anyone to vote and he was not a registered voter himself. He stayed away from our Freedom School because he was afraid he would be asked to help with the instruction of

The Freedom House in Valley View just after a rain.

others. We finally had a meeting with the COFO (Council of Federated Organizations) office. Our area in Madison County was administered by the Congress of Racial Equality (CORE). Dave Dennis was the main person in charge. Dave came to Valley View and saw our living conditions. He also noticed that Carolyn , a volunteer from California, and I were living together in the Freedom House. He told me he "didn't want any freedom babies" and gave me a box of condoms.

After our discussion, which included an in-depth discussion of the goals and strategies of our project, Andy and I became co-directors of the Valley View project. I was placed on Congress of Racial Equality (CORE) staff and received $14 per week. We worked closely together, he with his excellent contacts in the local community, and me with a vision and strategy to continue Freedom Schools, encourage voter registration, elect delegates to the Mississippi Freedom Democratic Party (MDFP), and organize black farmers, farm workers, and sharecroppers to participate in the Agricultural Stabilization and Conservation Service

(ASCS) elections. We made a good team the rest of the summer and through the fall.

My parents visited Valley View in August of 1964. They were the only parents I saw that summer who visited their children, showing their love and support for the civil rights movement and their children. I introduced my parents to everyone in the Valley View neighborhood. My father, upon meeting several men, said, "Hello Boys." He immediately realized that he had demeaned the men and apologized. My father referred to his friends in Illinois as "boys" and his use of the word was an attempt at being familiar and friendly. In Mississippi and the South, black men were often called "boy" even though they were adults and responsible family men and respected members of the black community. He was horrified that he had used a pejorative term for the men he met. The men he met said nothing, but smiled and shook his hand. I quickly assured him that no damage was done, but it was a watershed moment for him. He stopped using "boys" to refer to anyone, even his own friends.

Initially, there was a pay phone in the living room. An AT&T worker came often to empty out the coin box, as it was in constant use. Even though we were cordial and kind to this man, he appeared to be very uncomfortable when he serviced the phone. It wasn't long before he removed the phone, telling us that it did not pay the phone company to maintain the phone in such a remote location. Removal of the phone left us with no way to contact anyone who was beyond shouting distance. We felt vulnerable but we had no alternative. We had to rely on our constant vigilance and the protection of our neighbors.

We organized a constant lookout for suspicious cars, trucks, and people. We had a posted schedule for people to serve as a lookout all day and all night. We generally followed this schedule, but it was common for others to keep the watch person company during the early morning hours when little was going on. Lead slugs imbedded in the trim around the front door were a constant reminder that we were subject to attack anytime, night and day.

My sister Kay.

Some civil rights workers lived with local people in their homes. These local homes had only one wall of boards that served as both the outside and inside wall, and every house was heavily lined with newspapers on the inside walls to provide more privacy and keep out the wind.

None of these rural homes had running water or indoor plumbing. Few had electricity. This kind of living arrangement was a new experience for most of the volunteers, but I had been born into a home without running water and electricity. I grew up taking a bath in the middle of the kitchen floor in a galvanized tub. The living arrangements in the Freedom House were not unknown to me, and were a reminder that so called modern conveniences such as running water were really not needed in order to survive.

My sister Kay described her accommodations in a similar nearby rural area. She wrote, "Karol and I shared the front bedroom of the Wiggins' house. This house had no indoor plumbing. Water came from a well beside the back door and cheesecloth hung on a bush for filtering out the big stuff. We bathed in a #3 galvanized wash tub (Karol took a picture of me in it) and when we grabbed the TP and headed for the outhouse, a line of chickens followed and inspected the open back of said shack.

Mrs. Wiggins served fried chicken every Sunday."

Kay continued, "We shelled peas, held babies, and attended lots of church mass meetings at which we always heard the remark, 'You are the first white folk who ever called me Mr. or Mrs.'" Kay said, "I truly enjoyed living in the black community. No one refused to take me seriously because of my gender. It was no accident that the three candidates for the Mississippi Freedom Democratic Party (MFDP) were women. Individual differences were celebrated. For the first time I felt that I did not have to fit into a mold to be accepted."

In the Freedom House at Valley View there was a gas stove just for cooking. On cold mornings, our gas oven served as a heater for the entire house. The gas stove was also our water heater for bathing. The most common "bath" was a bucket bath. A bucket bath consisted of heating a bucket of water on the stove to tepid, dunking your head into the water and shampooing and rinsing your hair, then washing your limbs and torso.

Charles taking a shower he made from a five gallon lard can.

A young man uses the slim "bucket" to draw water from the well.

At first, it seemed like everyone had to fend for themselves, even though we lived and worked together. There seemed to be little organization and planning, although some staffers did drive into Canton a couple of times each week in order to purchase food and supplies. I rarely went into town, as there was always a lot to do on the project. I felt a part of this community because we were engaged in the battle for respect and dignity in the quest for basic civil rights for the citizens of Valley View. But I felt closer to the local citizens, because they were the real reason I was there. The local people became my friends and chosen people to hang out with. I felt more integrated into their community than that of the civil rights workers. I began to receive invitations to stay for dinner or to go to church with local families. I almost always accepted these welcomed chances to mingle with and become a part of the local community. I felt safe and accepted with my new friends in the black community.

In the office, we had a shortwave radio transceiver, and mobile units in a few of the cars. In order to be effective, there needed to be a person in the office monitoring the radio. And if there was a problem, that meant that only the person at the Freedom House knew about it. Without a telephone, no calls could be made to contact any emergency services. And who could we call? The local sheriff was no help, and the nearest FBI office was in Jackson, over fifty miles away. This radio was the only way we could keep in touch with anyone while we were out in the community.

We had some supplies, including felt tipped pens and cardboard. It was with these few supplies that we waged our war against the racist white power structure in Madison County, Mississippi, by targeting discrimination in voter registration, school segregation, organizing the Mississippi Freedom Democratic Party (MFDP), and black farmers in a campaign to gain representation on the local Agricultural Stabilization and Conservation Service (ASCS) boards.

Each day began with a search for food, water, a bathroom, people, and something to do to further the struggle for civil rights. Each day was a new adventure. For example, we would

Charles and children building an outhouse.

A volunteer and a child take a bath in a pond in a pasture.

get up and look for a place to pee. That seems insignificant, but without any bathroom or other facilities, it can be problematic, especially when it was raining or cold or both. When I first arrived, I just crawled over the fence and went behind a tree, as did everyone else.

One of the first things I did was to try and fix the plumbing in the Freedom House. This was one of the only houses in the entire area with an indoor bathroom, complete with commode and tub. But without running water, it all was useless. I found that the pump from the shallow well did not work, and that seemed to be the problem. I removed the pump and found a local repair shop. In a couple of days, the pump was ready to be reinstalled. I put the pump back in operation, only to discover that all the pipes leaked. I spent hours trying to stem leaks in faucets, pipes, and connections between the fixtures. After the pump failed for the third time, I abandoned the pump and any attempt to provide running water in the Freedom House.

With no water for either the kitchen or the bath, we had to find other means for washing and bathing, and for basic bodily functions. I began to search the neighborhood for materials which could be used for these purposes, including building an outhouse for the volunteers.

There was a well between the Freedom House and the little country store. It was a six inch pipe sunk in the ground about thirty feet. The water table was fairly high, so we never ran out of water. The "bucket" was a long tube about five inches in diameter with a valve at the bottom which permitted water to flow into but not out of it. The bottom valve leaked so badly, that you had to be quick in pulling up and dumping the water before it all leaked out. This bucket was about four feet long and was suspended by a pulley over which a small chain ran, and was attached to the top of the bucket.

A few weeks later, I found some old wood planks and posts that were apparently abandoned. I built an outhouse from this scrap lumber I found in the neighborhood. This lumber was

Charles taking a shower and other volunteers washing clothes.

Local women doing laundry by hand.

weathered and full of knotholes and appeared to be of no use. I sunk four poles in the ground and nailed the boards to them, creating a three sided structure with a roof. I dug a deep trench for depositing our waste. In addition to various boards, I found an old seat from a former outhouse. We used this for its original purpose. This was a welcome option from going out behind the Freedom House in a pasture. This arrangement worked well until the rains came in the fall. Then everything floated out from the trench and made a mess of the side yard.

To make a shower, I used a five-gallon lard can, and punched several holes in the bottom with a nail to let water run out. I hung this "shower" from the frame that was constructed around the well, which supported the chain attached to the bucket for drawing water from the well. We would dump a bucket of water from the well into the lard can and take a shower with our bathing suits on. The shower was in the open, so we had to wear a swimming suit to cover our bodies. The water was pretty cold,

The "finished" outhouse, being admired by volunteers.

but we were glad for the opportunity to take a shower instead of a bucket bath or going to a nearby pond in a pasture for bathing.

We took turns cooking food that members of the local community donated. The food was mostly vegetables and other food grown from their gardens and farms. But they were so poor we tried to discourage their gifts. This was difficult, because everyone wanted to show their appreciation of our being in their community and trying to make changes in their lives and in the social, economic, educational, and political fabric of life in Madison County, Mississippi.

One issue that emerged early on was the need for doing laundry. A couple of local teens offered to do our laundry. Some of the volunteers accepted but when these enterprising teens began washing their clothes by hand, some of the volunteers relented. These volunteers told the teens that this was just the kind of activity we were trying to change, that of a person doing what another person did not want to do.

This did not go over well with the teens, as they saw this as an opportunity to make some money. Some volunteers said they thought the teens were going to use a clothes washer, not do the laundry by hand. None of the homes in the neighborhood had washing machines.

At the beginning of the summer, the local economy was pretty spartan. There was little, if any, excess cash in anyone's pockets. When the civil rights volunteers made their economic presence felt, that changed in a big way. These northern students were used to living in communities with a lot of resources, not in a rural community that relied upon sharing produce from locally grown gardens. The economy expanded with the influx of the volunteers and their resources. Local people began to find ways to economically benefit from these volunteers by doing odd jobs, fixing cars, doing errands, nearly anything that needed doing.

D: Freedom Schools

Freedom Schools were the rallying point, the meeting place for the black community during the summer of 1964. Schools were held anywhere there were people and a place to meet, including churches, old buildings, or even under a tree. The curriculum was as varied as were the students. There were students in all grade levels, from pre-school, through high school, college preparatory, and adults. Everyone was welcome, and everyone came. Freedom Schools were true community schools. They were supported by the community, attended by the community, and reflected the needs of the local community.

Brown vs. Board of Education, a landmark decision of the United States Supreme Court handed down on May 17, 1954, declared state laws establishing separate public schools for black and white students unconstitutional. The decision overturned *Plessy vs. Ferguson of 1896*, which allowed state-sponsored segregation, termed "separate but equal." Chief Justice Earl Warren's Court

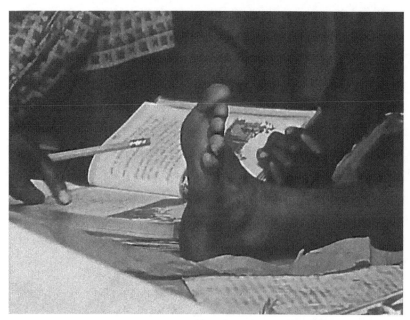

A scene from our Freedom School. Many children had no shoes.

issued a unanimous decision that stated "separate educational facilities are inherently unequal." As a result, de jure racial segregation, that which was authorized and prescribed by state and local laws, was ruled a violation of the Equal Protection Clause of the Fourteenth Amendment of the United States Constitution. This ruling paved the way for desegregation and helped empower the civil rights movement.

Attending school was not economically feasible for children of sharecropper families. Children in Mississippi were needed by their families, and by the white landowners, to plant, chop, and pick cotton. Children could earn their keep by picking cotton for two dollars per hundred pounds of cotton, a real feat for a child. I know that because I picked cotton with sharecropper families and gave my pickings to the children. Entire families spent months in the fields tending King Cotton. Making a meager living was far more important than learning to read and write. Children were hungry and needed to be fed, even if they had to help earn their own living. This was the stark reality still

A young child, hardly taller than the cotton plants, picks cotton in 1964.

Some students came to Freedom School by wagon and mule.

imposed by the Jim Crow laws on black families throughout Mississippi and the South.

In 1964, all the schools in the state of Mississippi were segregated. The black schools were in session about four months out of the year, and the white schools were in session nine months of the year. The reason for this disparity was that black children were expected to be in the cotton fields with their parents. White children did not share that burden. As a result, black children got a substandard education, whereas white children were given the full benefits of a public education. Most of the students and parents we served at Freedom School had undeveloped or underdeveloped basic skills for reading, writing, and mathematics.

I visited a black public elementary school with a black school board member as our guide, who was also a local cotton farmer. The school had no library and very few textbooks or books of any kind. The structure was wood framed with linoleum floors and painted walls.

Children at our Freedom School in 1964.

There were few desks and no visible supplies, including no chalk for the chalk boards and no erasers. Our guide told me that they used rags to erase the boards. The building needed paint on the outside and the inside needed blinds or shades to cover the windows. There were no frills but only the most basic of necessities. There was no indoor plumbing but there was a well for water. There were outhouses for students and teachers alike to use.

We were there when school was not in session. Nearly all the students were picking cotton, as were the children of the school board member giving us the tour. In spite of the substandard conditions of the school and the lack of supplies, this school board member and local leader was proud of this school. He had attended this school, as had his wife and all four of their children. Regardless of the condition of the school and the lack of supplies, it was the only school he and his family had ever known. This man was quite mindful of the disparity of education between white and black schools, and foresaw the day when his children could attend the well equipped white schools that had labs, gymnasiums, and cafeterias. But until that day, this was their school and they did all they could to make it as good a school as it could be with the scant resources at their disposal.

Freedom Schools in Mississippi were designed to serve the local community, including children and adults. These schools were designed to address the disparity of educational opportunity in the black community. The parents of the children who attended the Freedom School were also the product of a poor education. In 1964, the year of the Mississippi Freedom Summer, the state of Mississippi had done nothing to address the issue of substandard education for people of color. More importantly, there was no effort to comply with the U.S. Supreme Court's decision in *Brown vs. Board of Education*.

That meant that the parents of the children we served could not read or write at an acceptable level as a result of a very poor public education. As a result of our programs in Freedom Schools, adults got the opportunity to further their basic education.

Our Freedom School was in an old church.

Students discussing works of art at a Freedom School.

We conducted literacy programs for adults, including writing and reading. We also conducted programs in vocational training. This project enabled the students, including parents who learned these skills, to market them in their local community.

Our Freedom School was at a church with several dilapidated buildings around it which were pressed into service. One of these buildings was once an old school, but the windows were broken out. We replaced the windows and made it into a library. We gathered donated books from the community and our contacts in the North. We made bookshelves from old boards and stocked them with books and magazines. For many of our students, this was the first library they had ever seen. They were not allowed to use the all white county library, and their local school, for blacks only, had fewer books than the Freedom School library.

Our day at Freedom School was interspersed with other activities. We played basketball and other group games. We had discussions of current events, especially on topics of racism and black history. We obtained copies of great works of art and

Girl at Freedom School watches other children play.

discussed why they were considered important. We introduced different philosophies and tried to illustrate their applicability to our constitutional form of government. One example was "Life, Liberty, and the Pursuit of Happiness" in the Declaration of Independence, from the philosopher John Locke. We talked about how this influenced the writing of our Constitution and what it meant for our society.

Freedom Schools were open to all. At least, that was the theory. On my first day on the job, I met Johnny. He had been expelled for fighting, but he refused to go home. After all, there wasn't much to do in the hot Mississippi summers for a six year old with an attitude, but fight. Johnny wasn't good at fighting, but he persisted in trying. The other kids saw him as a minor bother, as no one had a bloody nose from Johnny. He was seen as a disruption by the teachers at the Freedom School, and was told not to return. He refused to comply. He really had nowhere else to go, as his older siblings were at school, and his parents were working.

Child writing at our Freedom School.

The recruitment of teachers for the Freedom Schools netted a lot of certified teachers. Two of the teachers in our Freedom School, Angelina and Karen, were from San Francisco, where they taught in the public schools. They were determined to run an orderly school and would not tolerate any student who would not be part of their orderly process of education. They were doing a good job of designing and implementing a varied curriculum with few resources. Everyone cooperated except Johnny and me.

Angelina and Karen ran a tight ship in the Freedom School, wanting it to mirror the type of classroom they had in San Francisco. They were very organized with detailed lesson plans and activities for everyone who attended Freedom School. They ran their classes as if it was a formal school and were intolerant of any deviation in their plans. They wanted strict discipline and insisted upon a rigid classroom. This was adhered to by most students, but some were less than cooperative. Most of the other teachers were less strict about behavior and attendance and were flexible about their curriculum when it came to the perceived needs of the students.

I took Johnny under my wing, literally. If left to his own devices, Johnny would spend the day tormenting all the other children. He would disturb classes by trying to pick a fight with someone. So I carried him. Fortunately, he was little. I couldn't get closer to anyone than his reach (swing), about two feet. Soon, Johnny agreed not to hit anyone, if I would let him walk. I agreed, and he kept his part of the bargain, usually. I think he enjoyed the attention he was receiving, so he would show a little aggression once in a while, just to see if I was still paying attention. I was.

The problem with Johnny became my problem with the teachers in authority and the reason for the existence of Freedom Schools. The two teachers from San Francisco were devoted to teaching and civil rights, and to an orderly school with them in charge. I did not disagree with them, but I felt that the concept of Freedom Schools was to serve the entire black community, including Johnny. It was up to us to adjust to whatever conditions we found, including unruly children. So I carried Johnny around, and kept him out of trouble. This rankled the teachers in charge, who felt that their authority was being challenged. I explained my concept of Freedom Schools, that they were for everyone, and that conventional ideas of education were really secondary to their purpose of including everyone in the civil rights struggle. The teachers explained how they felt about having their classes disrupted. But because I had successfully kept Johnny out of trouble by carrying him, the decision was made to let Johnny continue attending as long as he kept out of trouble. The teachers were upset, but everything worked out in the end. Johnny became a model student, and I became his friend. He eventually promised to stop fighting altogether, and he kept his promise.

The lesson plans we prepared for Freedom School included academic exercises as well as activities designed to entertain and amuse. We planned games with academic bases, such as spelling words or filling in missing words in a sentence in order to score points for a team of students. We tried to make learning fun by integrating games into our curriculum.

We also had to plan for the adults who were attending Freedom School. We usually met one on one with the adults and gave them individual instruction that targeted their specific needs. The learning gaps were varied from not knowing enough words to read a newspaper to not knowing how to form the letters of the alphabet. It seemed ironic to many of the volunteers that an adult could be successful as a parent and as a business person without knowing basic academic skills. When reflecting upon the experience of being a Freedom School teacher, some of the volunteers gained a new appreciation and respect for those adults who were apparently successful in raising children and making a living without ever learning how to read and write.

We worked hard on planning lessons that would engage our students. We planned fun activities as well as academic exercises, including softball and basketball games. We installed a hoop on a tree and many hours were spent on our new basketball

We played basketball with a hoop on a tree.

John proofreading a copy of the "Pleasant Green Magazine."

court. However, the academic activities were our main thrust. We spent hours pouring through our limited library looking for ways to enhance the limited English and math skills for all of our students. We had our students write about their daily lives and their aspirations in life. We also published a newspaper that was solely the work of our students, the "Pleasant Green Magazine." This popular work was the brainchild and effort of John, our representative in the Boston Marathon. It contained poetry, news, history, riddles, and stories. One example of an original riddle in the magazine: I am tall and fat and have green hair, sometimes brown. When I was little I lost my suitcase, but when I grew up, I got a trunk. I have a hundred arms. What am I? Answer: A tree.

We had students of all ages, but one of our proudest accomplishments included tutoring a student for the SAT, Joe Williams. He obtained admission to the College of Emporia, in Emporia, Kansas, plus a scholarship. He had never been out of Mississippi,

Joe Williams (wearing a hat) sings at Freedom School.

or even Madison County. Joe Williams became the first person from the black community to attend college out of state. He was self effacing and very quiet and did not believe that he would ever go to college. I remember when he left Valley View in a car with other civil rights workers. He had said his goodbyes to his family, but there were still tears in his eyes. He was realizing the impossible dream for a black man in 1964 from Mississippi, attending college on scholarship.

Mr. Otha Williams began attending Freedom School and received individual instruction from Phil. He progressed quickly and his communication skills improved to the point of his being able to read the newspaper and fill out orders for his store. He did not try to hide his lack of education, but realized it was from the segregation in the public schools and the agrarian economy that forced entire black families to work in the fields. Mr. Williams embraced the opportunity for self improvement offered by the Freedom School. His open involvement led other adults to seek similar instruction.

All the teachers met at the end of each school day to plan the approach for our next day of activities and instruction. These meetings included an assessment of perceived needs from the current day and suggestions for addressing these needs in the curriculum for the next day and succeeding days.

For example, a chronic problem was the lack of materials. We might need twenty copies of an article or essay to hand out to the students. Without a copier (not yet available) we would type a mimeograph "master" and run copies on a hand crank mimeograph machine. We had to keep such requests to a minimum since the "masters" were in short supply. Then we had to collate and staple the copies by hand. Often we had the students assist in this process, much like the publication of the "Pleasant Green Magazine."

Often, a particular student had a unique learning issue not shared by the rest of the students. We tried to address individual problems with one-on-one tutoring and assignments on specific issues. Usually, though, there were educational deficiencies

Civil rights workers collate copies of the "Pleasant Green Magazine."

Phil teaching a class in Freedom School.

shared by many students. One common problem was a limited vocabulary along with spelling of words with which the students were unfamiliar.

We made flash cards by hand that were used to teach word definitions and spelling for vocabulary that was new to our students. Much of what we did was remedial in terms of vocabulary for reading and writing. Due to the lack of access to books, most students were not aware of how certain words were spelled, even though these same words might be used daily in conversation. Our students were very good at recognizing the spoken word, but did not recognize that same word in a story or article. Through the use of our flash cards, repetition, and having our students use certain words in their writing, progress was swift. All of our students were excited about learning, and that process became its own reward. Students were proud to read aloud, and share their writing with other students.

This illustrates one of the unique characteristics of our Freedom School: Learning is its own reward. The ability to read and understand the written word, and express in writing one's own thoughts, feelings, and perceptions, was highly valued by our students. There was no need for rewards other than learning how to express oneself and being able to read and understand and assimilate the thoughts and ideas of others.

Our classes were small by today's standards, usually ten to fifteen students, often fewer. We tried to have everyone participate in every lesson. At the beginning of a class, we would put forth the theme or goal for that class. Then we would show how this particular skill was used in our daily lives in order to show and give relevance to the lesson. We would embark on the lesson by writing on a chalk board, reading from a book, or handing out copies of an essay or article for the students to read. After reading or hearing the article or essay, we would discuss the definitions of particular words and how their use enriched that piece of writing. The students were very perceptive about written and verbal expression and their comments greatly enriched our discussions. After about an hour, we would try to summarize the

Teaching typing to Mrs. Hattie McCullough at Freedom School.

lesson and especially the contributions of our students.

After receiving the donation of several manual typewriters, the Freedom School staff designed a typing class for anyone who wanted to learn this skill. Learning to type gave the person a marketable skill and assisted them in activities in their church and community.

Our students would tell others who were not in a particular class about new words and definitions they learned. It seemed that our students became teachers as well, often more effective than we teachers were. The Freedom Schools were truly learning communities. The hunger for knowledge and academic skills was self sustaining. And our students took their new found knowledge home with them to their parents and families. On more than one occasion, a parent or sibling would come to Freedom School and inquire about becoming involved after being exposed to an expression by a student. As a teacher in Freedom School, the positive learning environment was a great

Students singing at our Freedom School.

reward, making all of our work seem relevant to us as teachers and to the community we served.

Success of the Freedom Schools should be measured, in large part, by how many students attended. Keep in mind that the environment of the students from the black community was one of murder and beatings by police, no right to vote, no right to go to public schools, no civil rights at all. For a family to even participate in Freedom Schools put them at risk of being fired, firebombed, shot, beaten, or almost anything you can imagine. Working as a civil rights worker in Mississippi in 1964 was like working and living in a war zone. In this environment, it is invalid to look at the curriculum and any scholastic achievements. There are only anecdotal records of the Freedom School we organized and ran, but these are powerful indicators of the engagement of our students in the learning process.

The main and most extensive archive of material and information about the Freedom School at Valley View is Richard Beymer's movie, "A Regular Bouquet." In this movie, there is a discussion by Phil and John about the Freedom School and their roles as teachers. John also describes the "Pleasant Green Magazine" and the contributions of the students. There are scenes of students, including adults, involved in instruction, and scenes of group activities including games and basketball.

E: The Mississippi Freedom Democratic Party and Voter Registration

Registering to vote (reddish to vote, as the local people would say) was not a safe and easy process. Upon entering the courthouse, a black citizen might be arrested for trespassing on public property. Even if a black citizen was allowed to enter the office of the registrar of voters, he or she might wait in line for eight or nine hours and not even be spoken to.

The process of registering to vote was long and complicated. One part of the process was to copy a section from the Mississippi Constitution onto a paper, and then give "a reasonable interpretation" of that section. There were over 200 sections of the Mississippi Constitution, and the registrar's decision as to whether or not your interpretation was reasonable was final and not appealable. There is a copy of this literacy test in Appendix III. It is unlikely that you or anyone can pass this test.

A mass meeting in Indianola as part of the organizing for the Mississippi Freedom Democratic Party (MFDP).

In the example of the literacy test provided, there are twenty-one questions, most of which are personal information. In addition to being asked to interpret a section of the Mississippi Constitution, the applicant is also asked, "Write in the space below a statement setting forth your understanding of the duties and obligations of citizenship under a constitutional form of government." Whatever a black applicant would write, it would likely be rejected by the white registrar as inadequate. One of the sample sections of the Mississippi Constitution to interpret was section 209, "Separate schools shall be maintained for children of the white and colored races."

Mississippi was just one of the southern states to require a literacy test for black citizens to register to vote. Some examples from the Louisiana test (Appendix III) are the following:

1. Draw a line around the number or letter of this sentence.
2. In the space below, write the word "noise" backwards and place a dot over what would be its second letter should it have been written forward.
3. Place a cross over the tenth letter in this line, a line under the first space in this sentence, and a circle around the last the in the second line of this sentence.
4. Draw a figure that is square in shape. Divide it in half by drawing a straight line from its northeast corner to its southwest corner, and then divide it once more by drawing a broken line from the middle of its western side to the middle of its eastern side.

Not to be outdone, Alabama also had difficult, or impossible, literacy tests (Appendix III). Some examples are the following:

1. If election of the President becomes the duty of the U.S. House of Representatives and it fails to act, who becomes President and when?
2. How many states were required to approve the original Constitution in order for it to be in effect?

3. If it were proposed to join Alabama and Mississippi to form one state, what groups would have to vote in order for this to be done?
4. If the two houses of Congress cannot agree on adjournment, who sets the time?

We organized the Mississippi Freedom Democratic Party (MFDP) because the regular Mississippi Democratic Party (MDP) was as segregated as the whole state of Mississippi. Because of the discriminatory voting registration procedures, very few black citizens were able to register and vote anywhere in Mississippi. Mississippi had the worst percentage of black voters in the nation with only 6.7 percent of eligible black citizens registered to vote (*Shelby County vs. Holder,* U.S. Supreme Court, 2013). And not all of those black citizens voted because going to the polling place was fraught with danger for any black voter. Intimidation, beatings, and outright denial of the right to vote was all too common in Mississippi for all black citizens. This pattern of discrimination kept the Mississippi Democratic Party (MDP) in power.

Freedom Democrats attend a mass meeting.

Because black citizens were discouraged from registering to vote and from voting, the Mississippi Freedom Democratic Party (MFDP) was a viable alternative. If black candidates could be elected to offices statewide, this system would change. It was hoped that the Mississippi Freedom Democratic Party (MFDP) was the answer to disenfranchisement of black citizens in Mississippi.

The Mississippi Freedom Democratic Party (MFDP) was open to all citizens of Mississippi, not just the white population. The Mississippi Freedom Democratic Party (MFDP) delegation was the only integrated representative body from Mississippi to appear at the national convention of the Democratic Party. In addition, and this should have been the decisive factor in recognizing the Mississippi Freedom Democratic Party (MFDP) delegates, the MFDP was supportive of the nominee of the National Democratic Party, where the Mississippi Democratic Party was not. Lyndon Johnson, the party nominee, was spurned by the regular Mississippi Democratic Party, who went on to support the Republican nominee, Barry Goldwater.

In Appendix IV, there is a position paper, "Challenge of the Mississippi Freedom Democratic Party," which states that the entire state of Mississippi was tightly controlled by the regular Mississippi Democratic Party. All forty-nine senators and one hundred twenty-one of one hundred twenty-two representatives were Democrats, as was the governor and the judiciary. The regular Mississippi Democratic Party was open about its opposition to the National Democratic Party and its platform. They boasted, "Our Mississippi Democratic Party is entirely independent and free of the influence of domination of any national party."

The position paper provided by the Council of Federated Organizations (COFO) office in Jackson outlined the problems posed by the Mississippi Democratic Party. These included the systematic exclusion of black citizens from the political process, the lack of loyalty of the Mississippi Democrats to the National Democratic Party, and the intransigent determination of them

Mississippi Freedom Democratic Party (MFDP) candidates run for office in the general election of 1964 in Mississippi.

to keep and maintain the status quo of racism in Mississippi through the passage of Jim Crow laws. The Council of Federated Organizations (COFO) paper states that the Mississippi Freedom Democratic Party (MFDP) "is open to all citizens regardless of race."

There were four Mississippi Freedom Democratic Party (MFDP) candidates that qualified to run in the the June 2, 1964, primary election in Mississippi against the incumbent Mississippi Democratic Party candidates. Mrs. Victoria Gray ran against Sen. John Stennis. In 1964, Mrs. Gray was working as a door to door cosmetic saleswoman and voting registration activist. She felt that the regular Mississippi Democratic Party did not represent most of the people of Mississippi, whereas the Freedom Democratic Party was open to everyone. She lost the election, but helped promote the statewide system of Freedom Schools and encouraged registering to vote in the black community.

Mrs. Fannie Lou Hamer ran against Rep. Jamie L. Whitten. Mrs. Hamer tried to register to vote, only to be kicked off a plantation where she and her husband were sharecroppers. She became a Student Nonviolent Coordinating Committee (SNCC) member and a civil rights organizer. She is best known for her moving testimony before the credentials committee of the Democratic Party.

Rev. John Cameron ran against Rep. William H. Colmer. Rev. Cameron was pastor of the Second Baptist Church in Oxford, Mississippi. He later became pastor of the New Hope Baptist Church in Meridian, Mississippi. Meridian is where slain civil rights worker James Chaney and his family lived.

Mr. James Houston ran against Rep. John Bell Williams. All of the Mississippi Freedom Democratic Party (MFDP) candidates lost. The issues and the platform of the Mississippi Freedom Democratic Party (MFDP) included promoting anti-poverty programs, Medicare, aid to education, rural development, urban renewal, and the guarantee of constitutional rights for all. The Mississippi Democratic Party had no articulated platform, only the implied promise to continue to deny black citizens their constitutional rights, including the right to vote.

One of the main venues for organizing the Mississippi Freedom Democratic Party (MFDP) was Freedom Schools. We held "Freedom Days" at our local Freedom School. Our students, mostly school-aged children, told their parents to come to Freedom Days and register as a member of the MFDP. There were no literacy tests to try to pass, no poll taxes were required, and no people were on hand to harass or physically attack those who wanted to register as a Freedom Democrat. Freedom Days were a celebration of our community, our solidarity, and the resolve of each member of our community to show their support for change in our community. Nearly all of the local community attended and registered their support.

In addition to Freedom Days in our Freedom Schools during the summer, we also held local caucuses in churches, and a county assembly in Canton, the county seat of Madison County. At the county assembly, representatives to the state-wide convention were elected. Our local representative to the Democratic National Convention was Annie Devine. Mrs. Devine was a full time worker for Congress of Racial Equality (CORE), giving up her job in a local insurance office. She quickly became well known throughout Mississippi as a companion of Fannie Lou Hamer and Victoria Gray. These three fearless and determined women traveled the state making speeches and encouraging black citizens to get involved in the civil rights movement.

The national Democratic Party rules were followed as closely as possible, because the delegates who were elected planned on attending the Democratic National Convention in August which was to be held in Atlantic City, New Jersey. Sixty-eight delegates were chosen as representatives of the Mississippi Freedom Democratic Party for the entire state of Mississippi, as the only lawfully elected representatives of the Democratic Party in Mississippi.

On our project in Valley View, we signed up people who should be eligible voters as members of the Mississippi Freedom Democratic Party (MFDP). We recruited persons to serve as delegates to the Democratic National Convention. We also attempted to get representatives from our community to run for local offices in fall elections. But because of the lack of black voters in Madison County, there were few persons who even considered running as local candidates.

When the Mississippi Freedom Democratic Party (MFDP) delegation left for Atlantic City in late August, Richard Beymer and I were in Indianola and Ruleville filming the local Freedom Schools and mass meetings. We also stayed at the home of Fannie Lou Hamer and interviewed her. When she left for the bus to Atlantic City, New Jersey, for the Democratic National Convention, she told us we could remain in her home and watch the Democratic National Convention on her television from her living room. We did, and she was electric. Although the news accounts I have since read state that she told the news commentators, after being offered two at large seats at the convention, "We didn't come all this way for no two seats," but my recollection is she later said, "We didn't come all this way for no damn two seats."

Fannie Lou Hamer, a candidate and delegate of the Mississippi Freedom Democratic Party, was forced to leave her home because she tried to register to vote.

The testimony of Mrs. Hamer electrified the nation, so much so, that President Johnson interrupted her live interview with a news conference. The networks shifted away from Mrs. Hamer to cover the president. But her testimony was replayed and millions of Americans learned that Mrs. Hamer was a former sharecropper who, with her husband, had been thrown off the plantation where they worked because they had tried to register to vote.

F: Life in Valley View: Fall

When the summer came to an end and most of the volunteers returned home, nearly all of our activities and projects were curtailed. We stopped having large classes at our Freedom School, we cut back on trying to register people to vote, and after the Democratic National Convention in Atlantic City, we stopped our efforts at organizing the Mississippi Freedom Democratic Party. We did make efforts at keeping these activities alive by enlisting local persons to take leadership roles, which was our main goal from the beginning. At the end of the summer, our focus became organizing local black farmers for the Agricultural Stabilization and Conservation Service (ASCS) elections in early December.

Our fall planning took an entirely different route. We were almost totally isolated on the Valley View project with little contact with the Canton office or the main Council of Federated Organizations (COFO) office on Lynch Street in Jackson. We did have some general guidelines as to what we were to accomplish. We were to encourage people to register to vote. We were supportive of the Mississippi Freedom Democratic Party and our local representatives. We tried to maintain a semblance of continuity for our Freedom Schools, even though the black public schools were finally in session. We were beginning to organize the farmers for the upcoming elections for representation on local Agricultural Stabilization and Conservation Service (ASCS) boards. We were to encourage local involvement in these tasks, hopefully resulting in a leadership role of local people. The goal was to have the local people run the civil rights programs that were designed to benefit their local community, educational system, and economy. Our director, Andy Green, was important to the success of our many projects because he became an integral part of the local community and one of our strongest links to that community.

This left a skeletal staff, just two people in the Freedom House, Carolyn and me. Our evenings were spent hashing over the day's travails and making plans for the next day. We took

Carolyn and Charles handing out flyers about the ASCS elections to be held in the fall of 1964.

turns watching the road and the surrounding fields for anyone approaching the Freedom House so we wouldn't be burned out or shot by a passing car or sniper. I searched around the Freedom House most mornings. Several times I found unignited Molotov cocktails. It is a miracle that we were never burned out, and a greater miracle that our nearby country store was never burned, because I found broken gallon glass jugs with a burned wick in the weeds next to the store on several occasions.

Carolyn was from San Francisco, and came to Mississippi at the beginning of the summer. She and I worked mainly in the Freedom School during the summer, and turned our attentions to voter registration and organizing the farmers in the fall. We worked together for months organizing mass meetings, trying to get people to register to vote, and informing farmers and sharecroppers of their voting rights in the upcoming ASCS elections. Of course, at that time it was only trying to register to vote, as most efforts to register were unsuccessful.

Carolyn was about five feet tall and weighed one hundred pounds, but she was fearless when it came to mounting a crusade to change the social, educational, and economic status for black citizens of Madison County. She was very good at getting people to speak with her on these issues, a real feat, as many black people would not even look at or speak with whites at all. She was good at meeting these fears and charming the people she was trying to reach. Carolyn always had information and handouts that were very useful at imparting information as to the strategies we were trying to use to make much needed changes in the black community. She was a good talker and very serious about her job as a community organizer. She gained the respect of everyone she met, including the local sheriff.

Carolyn and I attended Sunday services at multiple churches. The churches were the main focus of our community organizing. Churches were a mainstay of the local community. Even though they were kind enough to give us some of their precious time after the service to tell parishioners what we were trying to do, several of the sermons I heard told the people to trust in the Lord, not in the civil rights activities we were there to promote. This difference in philosophy and action did not seem at odds with the people, as they continued to both participate in civil rights activities and attend church.

Some of the churches had services twice each morning with different people in attendance. Often there was also a prayer meeting in the evening for those who had attended another service at another nearby church. There was always a lot of food, fried chicken, salads, pies, and fresh produce from the many gardens in the community. There was a lot of socializing. Different groups formed including women, teenagers, farmers, kids, everyone feeling a part of an extended community. It was clear that there were many reasons for attending church, not all related to the sermon or the teachings of Christ.

One night, while conducting a meeting at a local church, a member of the sheriff's department walked into the meeting.

This man was the prior Madison County Sheriff and before his term was over, he had created a post called "sheriff at large" for himself. This man, Billy Noble, invoked fear and loathing on the part of everyone in the black community. Mr. Noble was rumored to be a member of the Ku Klux Klan, and the White Citizens Council. When he walked into the church, a hush fell over the people attending the meeting.

He brazenly interrupted our meeting and ignored everyone there, except the civil rights workers. He walked to the front of the church and told us that we were in danger. He suggested a different route for us to return to the Freedom House. He told us to take a little used country road instead of the main highway, U.S. 51. After the meeting, we returned by way of the main highway, instead of the route he suggested. We did not take his advice, and we returned home safely. Had we listened to him, we may not have returned at all.

We also had meetings at St. John's Baptist Church, a local church about a half mile from the Freedom House. At these meetings, we encouraged local black farmers to vote in the elections for representation on the local boards that administered federal programs for farmers. The federal government has a lot of programs to encourage farming and farm production. These programs are administered on a local level by the locally elected boards. In order to vote in these elections, a farmer or sharecropper only had to show that he or she was engaged in agriculture. Since it was a federally based program, restrictive Mississippi state laws governing voter registration did not apply. That meant that black farmers could vote in these elections without being forced to take literacy tests or interpret the Mississippi State Constitution.

We organized workshops to help inform local people how to register to vote in both the regular elections and the federally run elections for representation for farmers. We provided information on how the community could benefit from voting in regular elections as well as the Agricultural Stabilization and Conservation Service (ASCS) elections that were held for

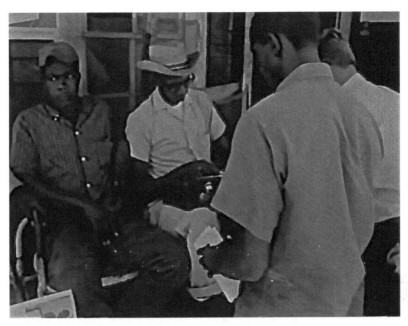

Canvassing for voters at a country store.

landowners and sharecroppers who were farmers. Most of the people and families were farmers. Some owned their land but most were sharecroppers.

We were usually welcomed by everyone we met in the community because by now there was a lot of trust which we earned over the summer. Each household had a story to tell about their struggle to live day to day, to find work, go to school, and survive the winter. Many people just lived off their parcel of land as best they could, tending their small gardens. Little was bought from a store. A family might get a pig and raise it for slaughter or have a cow for milk. Everyone went hunting for game. Some had a still for moonshine, others had cookers for sorghum cane juice used to make molasses. It all was part of the local culture which was very diverse.

Our strategy for organizing these local communities consisted of meeting at local churches with local citizens and offering to take them to the courthouse on a given day to attempt the voting registration process. We had to car pool with several cars to drive people to the courthouse.

At the end of the summer, there was a statewide meeting of all persons who had worked during the summer on voter registration and Freedom Schools. This was a retreat held at a resort on the Gulf of Mexico, in Waveland, Mississippi. This was the first time I was able to relax since my arrival in Mississippi several months earlier.

There were all the well known leaders of the civil rights movement in attendance, including Stokley Carmichael, Bob Moses, Jim Forman and Dave Dennis. Stokley Carmichael (Kwame Ture) was born in Trinidad, and attended Howard University in Washington, D.C. He grew up in New York City and became involved in the civil rights movement after seeing students sitting in at lunch counters. He was a Freedom Rider and was arrested for going into the white waiting room at the Waveland, Mississippi, bus station.

Bob Moses was the architect of the Mississippi Freedom Summer. He was from New York City, and had a master's degree in philosophy from Harvard. Bob was a reluctant freedom fighter, but felt it was a necessary evil because of the widespread racism throughout this country.

Jim Forman was born in Chicago and raised in Mississippi. He was about ten years older than most of the other civil rights organizers, but he was an integral part of the work of the Student Nonviolent Coordinating Committee (SNCC). He became the executive secretary of SNCC and was an effective voice for the civil rights movement.

Dave Dennis was the co-director of the Council of Federated Organizations (COFO), the main organizing arm of the Mississippi Freedom Summer. He is an attorney, a graduate of the University of Michigan Law School. He was one of the first Freedom Riders in 1961 and the Congress of Racial Equality (CORE) director for Mississippi. The State of Mississippi was divided up into SNCC and CORE regions, and I worked in a CORE region. Dave placed me on CORE staff and appointed me as co-director of the Valley View project in Madison County, Mississippi.

We had many daily meetings at Waveland, Mississippi. These were loosely organized and everyone had a right to speak and be heard. Of the many issues discussed, one, the position of women in the movement, was front and center. When this issue was raised, Stokley Carmichael (Kwame Ture) stood up and stated, "The position of women in the movement should be mainly prone," to the groans and chuckles of most of the persons at the meeting. His statement was immediately met with derision by the women supporting the dialogue. Stokley soon left the meeting, showing a lack of maturity and respect for the women in the movement who had sacrificed as much or more than anyone in that room that day.

The meetings were intense and everyone spoke. All topics were on the table. All decisions were made by everyone. Similar to the Student Nonviolent Coordinating Committee (SNCC), there was no "top down" hierarchy. But some speakers were more persuasive than others. Jim Forman and Bob Moses were particularly memorable. They prefaced their remarks with anecdotes and facts, then proceeded to lay out a thesis for future campaigns focused on tearing down Jim Crow laws, and building a stronger and more political black community.

Carolyn and I both attended the Waveland, Mississippi conference. Carolyn and I lived together in the Freedom House, worked together, and faced danger together. We were focused on our work in the community. We were also focused on each other, and we had an intimate relationship. But one day in late November, I returned from a local meeting to find Carolyn kissing a "former" boyfriend in the middle of the living room. This man, Jack, who was married with children, was from San Francisco. Carolyn had told me about him, but never suggested that he might actually appear in Valley View. When I walked in, she told me that she thought I would not mind, and that our relationship was not serious. I felt heartbroken and in shock. I contacted my sister Kay and she sent me the train fare from Canton, Mississippi, to Carbondale, Illinois. That is when I left the Valley View project, but not the civil rights movement.

G: Empowering Farmers

The Valley View project was in rural Madison County, Mississippi. In 1964, over sixty percent (60%) of the land owned in Madison County was owned by black farmers. Unfortunately, there were no black farmers on the advisory board. This meant that black farmers were prevented from receiving any federal monies for price supports, the soil bank, and other federal programs. In order to address this inequity, we decided to focus our attention on the elections for positions on this advisory board. This community of black farmers around Valley View had already built and operated their own cotton gin as a cooperative, but they were still denied attendance and representation on the local board that governed federal agricultural programs, including crop allotments for the most important cash crop, cotton.

The Agricultural Stabilization Conservation Service (ASCS), an agency of the United States Department of Agriculture, administered programs concerning farm products and agricultural conservation. It granted loans to farmers; purchased farm products from farmers and processors; administered land allotment and marketing quota programs; shared the cost of resource conservation and environmental protection measures with farmers and ranchers; and supervised civil defense activities relating to food. It also managed the inventories of the Commodity Credit Corporation. The ASCS was established in 1961 (U.S. Department of Agriculture).

Black farmers had not been represented on these kinds of boards since their inception. A farmer did not have to register to vote in the county courthouse in order to vote in these elections because they were operated by the federal government and were not subject to the racially restrictive voter registration laws and processes for state elections. Although all farmers and sharecroppers regardless of race were eligible to vote for the Agricultural Stabilization Conservation Service (ASCS) committee members, until 1964 all committee members in the

Deep South were white men.

Before the 1964 elections in Mississippi, the Council of Federated Organizations (COFO) began organizing black farmers in certain Mississippi counties that had established civil rights projects operating in them. Black citizens in these Mississippi counties ran for committee appointments, assisted by the Mississippi Freedom Democratic Party (MFDP), Congress of Racial Equality (CORE), Council of Federated Organizations (COFO), and the Student Nonviolent Coordinating Committee (SNCC). Although reports of voting irregularities and intimidation were widespread, some black citizens in Mississippi who ran for committee appointments were elected.

We in Madison County embarked upon a campaign to elect representatives to this board. We researched the boundaries for the various precincts and made maps that specified the names of the local roads that divided up Madison County into precincts for the ASCS elections. We also made available the information as to how and where a person could vote in these elections. We distributed that information to local farmers, sharecroppers, and others in agriculture, in local mass meetings. A sample of what we distributed can be found in Appendix V.

A mass meeting was considered very successful if ten people attended. We managed to get upwards of fifty people to most of our meetings by advertising them at Sunday services at local churches, many of which were the sites of the meetings. I placed the maps I had drawn of each precinct in churches in that area where we held informational meetings about the elections and their implications for black farmers. The maps were often propped up against the podium where the preacher stood when delivering his sermons.

In all the times I visited these various churches, and there were many, I always saw the maps I had drawn still occupying the central location in the front of the church as a reminder to everyone. Our strategy included identifying the precincts that comprised the areas where elected representatives would decide who received federal support. Our hope was that farmers attending those churches would see those precinct boundaries and know where to vote in that election. Apparently, it worked!

Parishioners were mindful that their church could be burned by the Ku Klux Klan and/or the White Citizens Council, or by local racists, simply for having a civil rights meeting there. Often, after the meetings, we discovered that nails were scattered on the roads leading from the churches. We began to regularly inspect the roads before leaving the churches.

One afternoon I had the opportunity to visit a local cotton gin with a farmer, Mr. Parrish. This was a cooperative adventure that the local black farmers had embarked on. They owned this operating gin. I rode on the seat of a four wheeled wooden wagon next to Mr. Parrish, pulled by a pair of mules. This wagon was like a buckboard with wooden wheels, the kind seen in old cowboy movies. These slow but sure mules were used by most farmers in this area.

Mr. Parrish was understandably worried about being seen with me going to the cotton gin. He was very self-conscious about the difference in the colors of our skin and the possible reprisals he could suffer from being associated with a civil rights worker. As we sat on that wooden bench behind the plodding mules, we talked about what changes were happening in the state of Mississippi. This man was a successful farmer, supporting a family and purchasing his own land. But we both were apprehensive about traveling along on the side of the public road in a slow-moving wagon which could easily be a target from a moving car. As we got closer to the cotton gin, we started to relax, because the other men at the gin would stand for no foolishness from any white racists. The farmers who ran the gin had strong resolve, and they were armed. I think this is why nobody bothered them, because it was widely known that they would use whatever force it took to defend themselves, their families, their community, and their gin.

When we arrived at the gin, everyone was glad to see us. There was a lot of banter and friendly chat. In a few minutes, our wagon was unhitched from the team of mules, and taken to be unloaded of its cotton. This process took nearly an hour, so we waited with the men who ran the gin. Finally, the empty wagon was rolled out, and we hitched up the mules and started back to the farm. The trip home was much faster, because the wagon was unloaded, and the mules were heading for the barn. We were both glad that it had been a successful venture, and that we had met no white people on the road. It was interesting to feel like I was not an outsider when we were at the gin. I felt the sense of security from the men there, that they would defend me as well as themselves. Of course, the white people saw the friendly association between black and white people to be a threat to their status quo.

I know I felt much more comfortable when we returned to Mr. Parrish's farm. When we were out of the public eye, we could relax a little. We jumped down from the wagon, and went into the house for a glass of water. There was a bucket of cool water from the well sitting in the kitchen. Mr. Parrish picked up a dipper, and offered the first drink to me. We all drank from the same dipper. Then we went back outside, and unhitched the team of mules. We led them over to the barn, and unbuckled the harness. We lifted the harness off their backs, and hung it from pegs to dry the sweat in the shade of the barn. Then I led the mules through the gate and released them in the pasture. They were happy their day's work was over. They drank their fill of water, and wandered out into the pasture to graze.

Mr. Parrish and I spent the next hour talking about our trip to the gin and the future of black farmers in Madison County. He was optimistic that better times were ahead. He also expressed his feelings of admiration and respect for the civil rights workers who came to Mississippi to try and change the rampant racism in his state. Even though Mr. Parrish felt vulnerable during our trip to the gin, he was proud to be seen with me, as testament to his own courage and commitment to the civil rights struggle.

I picked cotton with local black sharecroppers and families. We picked only those fields that were planted and maintained by local farmers, whether they were sharecroppers or landowners. Mr. Smith was one of the local sharecroppers, and I picked cotton in his field. Like nearly everyone, he wore bib overalls and wore a wide brimmed straw had. He had one good eye, the other permanently looking to the side. His scale, simply a large iron bar with marks for different weights, was hung from the side of his pickup truck. The cotton bags in which we placed the cotton were about ten feet long, and were closed at one end by a clasp. We dragged these long bags behind us as we went up and down the rows picking cotton.

Cotton is picked when the boll opens and dries out, exposing the cotton. The boll has sharp points that cut your fingers as you pick the cotton from the plant. After a few minutes, the cotton you place in your bag is streaked with your blood. Cotton is very light in weight, which is the reason for the long bags. They need to hold a lot of cotton in order for the picker to amass enough to weigh a few pounds. It takes 500 pounds of cotton to make one bale. There are stories and songs that tell of a person picking a bale of cotton a day, but that is a very difficult task. I picked about 100 pounds of cotton a day, and I thought I was doing well. Good cotton pickers picked about 200 pounds a day. They moved fast between the rows and filled their bags in an amazingly short time. They often had children bring them empty bags so they could keep picking and not waste time taking their full bags to be weighed.

Mr. Smith would hook the bag on his scale, rolled up so it did not touch the ground. He then would look at where the mark was that apparently told the weight. He then would call out the weight and enter it into his book. I never saw or heard anyone dispute his weights or his figures. I wondered if he really could see well enough to tell what the weight was, as he looked sideways at his scale. It seemed to me like he was looking into the woods, not at the scale. But he was trusted by all the other pickers and they had a very good idea of the weight of their pickings, so apparently Mr. Smith and their estimates were pretty close.

Almost everyone who was able-bodied picked cotton. There were children aged six or seven years old in the fields, along with their parents and grandparents. The cotton fields were often the only place to make contact with the local community during harvest season. I tried to talk to the people as we all labored in the sun. Usually they responded, but it was clear that this was serious business, and a time when everyone in the black community had a chance to make some money. The opportunity to make money trumped more theoretical concepts like civil rights and trying to register to vote. The best time to talk was when we rested in the shade for lunch, or during a short break from the scorching sun.

Picking cotton is backbreaking work. There is no shade and the sun seems to beat down on the cotton fields all summer. Everyone wore wide brimmed hats and long sleeved shirts to guard against

Picking cotton in Madison County, Mississippi in 1964.

Whole families picked cotton in order to earn a few dollars a day.

the sun's burning rays. In order to pick the cotton, the picker had to stoop over, as the cotton was usually about thirty inches from the ground. In just a few minutes, your lower back was begging to be straightened. Imagine walking for twelve hours, sun up to sun down, in the blazing sun, dragging a long bag that snagged on every bush, rock, root, or other obstacle, bent over at the waist, hands bleeding, picking the soft cotton balls as fast as you can, and thrusting them into the bag that seemed to be trying to strangle you as you walked.

There were no "porta potties," no water provided, no food. I had to find a tree or an overgrown fence row to relieve myself. I carried my own water and food. Breaks were taken sparingly, as my goal as a picker was to amass as many pounds of cotton as possible in my long sack. Late in the day, many pickers sought out a bit of shade and were resting, eating, and drinking.

The fields where I picked were off dirt roads, really sandy dirt. The soil was soft due to the sand. Sometimes it was like walking on a sandy beach where your feet slip on the sand and traction is limited. Every step forward takes greater effort because with each step I would slip back a bit. As the day progresses, the sun gets hotter, as does the air. The sun was also blinding and everything took on a washed out appearance. This environment was particularly hard on elderly pickers and children.

At the end of the day when the light had waned and the pickers had spent their energy, Mr. Smith totaled up the accounts for each picker. Wages were around two dollars per one hundred pounds of cotton picked, which is what I picked. At the time I was twenty years old in good physical condition but with little experience picking cotton. This surely was a very hard way to earn a living. As the weeks wore on, my efforts to increase my daily amount of cotton stayed about the same. It was a difficult job, very physical, under the hot sun. It was very hard for me to maintain the fast pace of experienced pickers who picked two or three hundred pounds a day, or more. It really took an entire family of four or more picking cotton all day to earn enough money to feed them all.

Some farmers also grew sorghum cane and used it to make molasses. One day I visited a farmer, Mr. Gary Williams, who was always wearing denim overalls and his wide brimmed straw hat. He was a big man with an easygoing manner. His smile was infectious, and everyone seemed to be his friend. When we first met, he made me feel like we had known each other all of our lives. His sense of humor kept the hard work of cutting the cane and feeding it through the grinders tolerable. Everything that was done on these small family farms was hard work. Everything was done by hand. If Mr. Williams wanted something done, he knew he had to do it himself. He had his own farm and grew a cash crop of cotton, and raised a few pigs for meat.

Mr. Williams had a stand of cane that he cut with a machete and piled it high. He had a grinder, actually two steel cylinders mounted on some steel girders that held them very close together. They were anchored over a vat which collected the cane juice that spilled out of the cane when it was fed between the cylinders. The whole contraption was powered by a small Ford tractor (8N) towing a large tree branch as a lever. The tractor went round and round, gouging a rut in the red dirt, and leaving a trail of oily exhaust. The lever turned some gears that linked both cylinders and made them both turn. It took a lot of force to turn them to grind and press the juice from the cane stalks.

Gallons and gallons of juice came out and it was poured into a large metal vat over a wood fire. The vat was divided up into channels. The cane juice was gently encouraged to go through the series of channels, something akin to a maze. As the juice made its journey, more and more water was evaporated and boiled off by the fire. The smell was tantalizing, a promise of the finished product, sweet molasses. The juice got more and more viscous and darker as it traveled through the maze. It was becoming molasses. The fire had to be hot enough to keep the temperature high enough to slowly boil off excess water. If it got too hot, the molasses would taste burnt. It was still good and could be eaten, but it was not the preferred product.

Richard Beymer sharing the sweet inner core of sugar cane with a child.

Making molasses was a community event. Many people showed up with their kids and dogs. Families mingled and children ran around, laughing and shrieking. Dogs barked, sometimes flushing out a rabbit, and the chase was on. The rabbit nearly always escaped.

Stories were told, recipes exchanged, and opinions shared. People shared news of community members who were away or in the military. If you listened carefully, you heard the same stories over and over again, told to a different audience.

Everyone wanted a taste of the sweet syrup as it came from the vat. Tastes were a common event, and everyone who sampled the product had their own opinion. And it got more complicated, as samples were taken all along the way through the vat, from different channels. That way, the taster could tell if the molasses was being cooked too hot, needed a little more fire, or was just right. Every taste was good, but some were emotive of poetry and exclamations: "That sure is the best batch this season!!" "That tastes a little burnt to me. Better damp down the heat some." "Pour in more juice to make it flow faster." "This sure will put a smile on Granny's face." "Can the baby lick the spoon?" "When can I fill my jar?" and "Damn, that molasses is GOOD!"

The vat and fire pit were in the woods, as all available and tillable land was planted in cotton and cane. There were no seats or benches. People dragged up fallen trees and stumps to sit on. Someone produced a guitar, and some singing began, mostly spirituals. It was a spontaneous celebration made possible by the closeness of the community.

The crushed stalks were fed to livestock. Even though they were tough, the animals liked the sugar and they were considered a treat. Stalks of cane were also chewed by the people standing around talking, gossiping, and smoking. All the children clamored for a new stalk to chew on, if theirs had lost its sweetness. A piece of cane stalk was peeled and the pithy inner core was chewed to extract the sugary juice. The cane was like cotton candy on the midway of a carnival. It was a festive atmosphere.

Richard Beymer cutting cane for Mr. Williams.

After the crowd left, Mr. Williams would damp down the fire and begin filling jars and jugs with molasses. This process took several hours and went in stages. First, the molasses had to be of the right consistency. It had to have the right color, not too dark, not too light. The darker molasses was called blackstrap. It was sometimes used as a medicine. It was somewhat bitter, but certainly good for you for sure, as everyone would attest. The lighter molasses was for pancakes and waffles. It poured well and was very tasty. All the in between molasses, different in color and viscosity, was eaten on sandwiches, baked in gingerbread, and made into a variety of baked goods, pies, stews (a little sorghum molasses is the secret) and nearly every dish that could use some sweetening up. One of the benefits of living in rural Madison County, especially Valley View, was sorghum molasses.

Most of the molasses was sold in the local community. Some made its way into George Washington's General Store in Canton. Some was on the shelf at Otha Williams' grocery store, also in Canton. A few jars were in the small county store near the

Freedom House. But most went directly to the consumer from Mr. Williams. Everyone wanted the best price. Some wanted it for free. But everyone wanted some. It was a seller's market.

We were engaged in grassroots community organizing with the farmers and the entire black community. We met with anyone who would speak with us about what needed to be changed in the educational, economic, political, and social structures of life in Mississippi, and how those changes might occur. The most important skill we needed was listening. We wanted the local people to tell us what their needs were and what local resources, to which they had no access, could fulfill those needs. We spoke with community leaders, often clergy, and nearly anyone in the community who would speak with us. It helped to have a local person canvass with us, as many people in the black community would not even open their doors to a white person.

The black farmers knew that they were being left out of the federal programs aimed at supporting farmers, but they had no strategy to obtain benefits for farmers like themselves. It took weeks and months of listening and talking, but we finally came up with a plan to educate the black farmers as to which precincts were electing representatives to the local boards that governed access to farm subsidies, what boundaries these precincts had, and how and where to vote in these special elections.

We passed out information about the Agricultural Stabilization and Conservation Service (ASCS) elections and different programs sponsored by the federal government designed to help farmers. These included price supports for crops such as cotton, corn, tobacco, and peanuts. Farmers and sharecroppers were told how these price supports worked and how they could get a guaranteed price for their harvest. But there were downsides, such as limiting the number of acres so that there would not be overproduction and a surplus of a certain commodity or crop. And there were alternatives to planting crops such as planting trees or not planting at all and putting land in what was called the soil bank.

Another program that would eventually prove quite popular with black farmers was the Commodity Credit Corporation, or the CCC. When enrolled in this program, farmers could store their crops and sell them later when prices improved. In the meantime, the CCC would loan the farmers money so they could continue their operations and not have to sell at a low price.

Each county in Mississippi had an Agricultural Stabilization and Conservation Service (ASCS) committee that made decisions about what federal monies were available, and how they would be allocated in the county. Every year, there were three candidates elected to this committee, and anyone who engaged in farming was eligible to vote. This included farmers, sharecroppers, tenants, landowners, and family members who were engaged in the activity.

In order to receive a ballot, each person had to register with the Agricultural Stabilization and Conservation Service (ASCS) office. In order to show that they were involved with agriculture, they needed to show a letter from the landowner, a deed to the land, a receipt for the purchase of seeds, farm machinery, or fertilizer. Many farmers would already receive a ballot, as they were recognized as farmers because they had some contact with the Department of Agriculture.

Finally, we had to put forth a slate of candidates. This was particularly problematic, as the black candidates were putting themselves and their families, friends, and their churches at risk, simply by having their names on the ballot. These candidates were also farmers in their respective areas. We continued having meetings at churches in various areas of Madison County that were part of the precincts in which the elections were to take place. When the votes were tallied, black farmers were represented on the Agricultural Stabilization and Conservation Service (ASCS) board in Madison County, the first time since Reconstruction.

One black farmer, Mr. Mills, was a very hard working farmer. When I urged him to register to vote he showed me his poll tax receipts for the past twenty years. He had them in an old Roi Tan cigar box. He had paid his poll tax all those years in the hope that he would someday be allowed to register to vote and vote for the candidate of his choice. He was a very successful farmer and owned his own farm. However, he had never been allowed to register to vote all his life. He was afraid for himself and his family. All black people who tried to register to vote were risking their lives and the lives of their families. But Mr. Mills finally did vote in the Agricultural Stabilization and Conservation Service (ASCS) elections and was proud to do so.

Phil worked with farmers in the southern part of Madison County, near the small town of Flora, Mississippi. He had a county map, as did we. Phil told me that the county was divided into sections with one Agricultural Stabilization and Conservation Service (ASCS) board member to be selected by ballot to represent each section. In Valley View we did the same. We both drew maps of each section of the county with every house on it, along with the local roads and their county names and local names.

Phil located a black farmer near Flora who agreed to be a candidate for the board. This was no easy task since most of the black farmers were illiterate. This farmer's name was Luther Honeysucker. Teaching these farmers who had never been taught to read or write to write in the name of Luther Honeysucker put Phil's teaching skills to the task. After choosing Mr. Honeysucker as a candidate and teaching the farmers to write his name, the next task was to be a poll watcher as the votes were cast and counted. Many of the ballots were illegible and were thrown out, but Mr. Honeysucker garnered enough votes to be elected to the board. He was the first black farmer on the board.

Another local farmer was Mr. Payton, a relative of NFL Hall of Fame running back Walter Payton. During the Mississippi Freedom Summer, both Payton brothers, Walter and Eddie, were in grade school. Both brothers attended Jackson State College, an historic African American institution in Jackson, Mississippi. They both later played in the NFL. Mr. Payton was a throwback to earlier days when people had forty acres and a mule. Mr. Payton had one mule and about forty acres. He was retired from the industrial Chicago area. He was very muscular and totally self-supporting. He only wanted to farm his land and be left alone. He was very friendly, but spent all of his time tending his farm. He hired no help and did everything himself. He was not the only Payton in the small black community of Valley View, but he exemplified the spirit of the community as one of independence and perseverance. Mr. Payton voted in the Agricultural Stabilization and Conservation Service (ASCS) election as well.

H: Our Community

Our "community" was several square miles in area, and we had to drive from farm to farm, house to house, church to church, field to field, in order to help organize the people. Using the shortwave radio, we kept in touch with each other when we were out canvassing for people who were willing to try registering to vote, or when attending community meetings, usually held at churches in the area. Canvassing for voter registration entailed speaking to people in the black community and telling them of their right to vote, which they already knew, and offering to take them to the county seat in order to begin the voter registration process.

The Freedom House in Canton was a small one story clapboard house with a small yard, across the street from the landlord,

FLASH!   *FLASH!*   *FLASH!*

Riders Throw Bomb At Freedom House

CANTON, MISS. - A bomb thrown from an automobile exploded outside the Canton Freedom House early Monday morning.

The bomb, thrown at the house, bounced off, rolled 20 feet away and exploded. The windows in the house were shattered. No one was injured. There were two people in the house at the time of the bombing, 1:30 A.M.

Later that night somebody called the Freedom House and asked "How many did we get."

The Freedom House has been under constant harassment from callers for the last few weeks."

Over 50 people were arrested and a Negro youth was beaten unconscious during a Freedom Day, here, May 29.

Canton, located in the 4th Congressional District, has been the site of a concentrated voter registration drive by the Council of Federated Organizations, a coalition of major civil rights groups in Mississippi.

Canton was a dangerous place for those who lived in the Freedom House.

George Washington, and his general store. Like most homes in the black community in Mississippi, this house was built with one single wall of boards. The outside of the house were boards which were not very close together. These outside boards were also the inside walls. In most instances, they were covered inside with newspapers glued to the walls to help keep out the drafts. There was no drywall or insulation. There was chicken wire on the windows. This was not for security, but to cause firebombs to bounce off. In Canton and Valley View, where I spent most of my time, people throwing firebombs or Molotov cocktails at our Freedom House was a fairly common occurrence.

My sister Kay, who also spent time in Canton, wrote to me, "All summer we avoided going out at night. We had to tape the interior light button down on the cars so that we would not be a lighted target. We stretched chicken wire over the Freedom House windows so that the bombs would bounce off, and they did. Many of the cars were equipped with two-way radios and a common practice of the Klan or White Citizens Council was to radio a distress call supposedly from a civil rights worker and set up an ambush. Pickups with full gun racks in the cabs drove by constantly, the drivers leering and making obscene gestures."

Kay continued with the following: "Our first night in Canton, we stayed with a family who had attempted to register to vote. As a result, both husband and wife had lost their jobs. In the hall was a crated bathtub which they had not been able to afford to install. They had no food in the house but they did have a fig tree in the back yard and we had delicious fresh figs for breakfast. They were truly regal." They said, "It is time for us to vote and we will not back down."

Kay continued, "... today Madison County's elected officials represent its majority black population. But in 1964, county officials were known to administer the written test for registering to vote in Chinese. One wag, when presented with this test and asked if he could read the Chinese version, replied, 'Sure I can read it. It says, 'Ain't no niggers gonna reddish today.'"

The Canton Freedom House had running water, electricity, and was connected to the city sewer. This was not the usual case, as most houses in the black community did not have indoor plumbing, water, or electricity. The Freedom House was not only a home for living, but the headquarters for civil rights activities in all of Madison County. Madison County had several projects, one in the northern part of the county, one in the southern part, and the main thrust in Canton, the county seat.

We were on the black side of town, where there were no curbs or sidewalks, and the streets were dusty. It felt like we had been transported into another time where nothing was modern and everything had stopped progressing around the turn of the century. That included police and fire protection, city services, and street maintenance. It also included the attitudes of the white population, including the police and fire departments, who would not miss a chance to insult or demean us if they thought we were "outside agitators."

There were two stores in Canton where we shopped. One was owned by our neighbor in Valley View, Otha Williams. Mr. Williams was one of the largest cotton farmers in the county, as well as an entrepreneur. The other store was owned and operated by George Washington. Mr. Washington's store had everything much larger chain stores had. The walls and ceilings were covered with merchandise suspended from hooks.

Both Mr. Williams and Mr. Washington were community leaders, fearless, and strongly committed to civil rights for everyone. They were an inspiration to the community, to civil rights workers, and to the Freedom School teachers. It felt good to be in the good graces of these respected men. Without that kind of local support from community leaders, we would not have been successful in our efforts at organizing the local community.

Otha Williams lived with his family on a farm in Valley View near our Freedom House, and he was a self-made man. He was tall and rangy, and always wore bib overalls with a wide

*Otha Williams, an
intense and brave man.*

brimmed hat. He had an infectious smile and an easy manner that masked an intense personality. As our nearest neighbor, he often stopped by to see if we needed anything. He was a businessman and a farmer. He concentrated on farming with cotton being his main cash crop. He tended to do everything himself, along with his John Deere tractor and implements. He was the first black farmer to own a mechanical cotton picker. It was called a one-armed picker, because it picked one row at a time. Mr. Williams was outspoken and fiercely independent, but he was a product of the segregated system of education in Mississippi. As a result, he could not read or write. He received instruction to improve his skills from our Freedom School teachers.

Otha Williams drove an International pickup truck. He noticed the trucks owned by the white farmers and "good old boys" all had gun racks in the back windows of their trucks, with their arsenal proudly displayed. Mr. Williams bought his own gun rack and had his guns in the back window of his truck as well.

It was widely known that anyone who would challenge Otha Williams was in for a fight, so no one ever did.

One day, Mr. Williams came by the Freedom House, and told me that his dog had been shot. He had a large collie mix that was feared by all. We found his dog dead and thrown off the bridge into the river. He was very upset that someone had killed his dog. This made him even more determined to change things in Madison County. If the white people had known that they were making unwanted changes happen more quickly by angering people like Mr. Williams and trying to cling to the past, they might not have been so aggressive and cruel toward their black neighbors.

Even though nonviolence was our method for confronting and dealing with violent racists in Mississippi, the local community was not. My sister Kay wrote: "While we were committed to nonviolence, the local people were not. I heard from another volunteer that a gun battle took place over a farm pond between her host family and some attackers. Every house I visited, especially in rural areas, had a rifle within easy reach of the door. A man in Madison County said he had been shot and left in a ditch several years earlier by a white acquaintance. He survived, but he kept a gun by every door and one in the car."

George Washington was one of the largest landowners in Canton, and the owner of one of the largest and best stocked general stores in the entire area. He was small of stature, big of heart, and always had a genuine smile and a comfortable manner. He was open about his commitment to civil rights. Whenever I entered his store, I always felt welcome. Mr. Washington always engaged in conversation about local or national issues, and he was well read. He sold newspapers from around the state and knew what was going on in all venues. He took the time to personally relate to whomever came into his store and made me feel like a personal friend. If I went to Canton, I always stopped to see Mr. Washington.

He rented one of his houses near his store in Canton to the Congress of Racial Equality (CORE) as a Freedom House. He

*George Washington of
Canton, Mississippi.*

seemed unafraid of anyone or anything. Sometimes, his properties were firebombed, as was the Freedom House. The insurance companies always investigated his claims because he was such a good customer and they could not afford to lose the business of the entire black community in Madison County just because they might object to Mr. Washington's stand on political and social issues. In this instance, at least, commerce and business interests trumped racism.

Mr. Washington was unflappable in his support for civil rights and did anything asked of him to support the movement. He was respected by the entire Canton community, including the white power structure. His openness and easy going manner belied a man who had an iron resolve regarding the issues confronting the black community. Regardless of your opinion on these issues, you had to respect Mr. Washington.

Becoming a part of the black community was essential for the survival of the volunteers. First, we needed to identify with a social structure to avoid feeling like outcasts or a hermits.

Second was protection. The community, though quiet, tender, and loving, took care of their own. An aggressive act against one person was seen as perpetrated against all people in the community. We, as civil rights workers, were part of this community, our extended family. The people in our community shared with us whatever they had, including game, sorghum molasses, moonshine, and protection. We were deeply appreciative.

To augment our diet, I went hunting several days each week. I often went hunting at night with local men from our community. They had hunting dogs, and we would track game like raccoons and possums and try to bring them back for food. Once in a while, we would come across a rabbit sitting in the woods, which soon became dinner for someone in our group. Hunting at night with dogs was both a form of socializing and survival.

Mr. Steven Williams, one of the hunters, had a dog named Red. She was a Redbone hound, and was the best tracker for miles around. Other men wanted their dogs to hunt with Red, so they could learn from her. Often we had a pack of six or more dogs on our hunts. No one had a gun, but I had borrowed a 16 gauge shotgun from a neighbor, so I carried the only firearm on our hunts. The men told me that they used to hit their prey on the head with a club before I accompanied them with a shotgun. I bagged rabbits, possum, and other game on our hunts.

When local men and I spoke with each other during the day, we planned our hunt in the woods after dark. We would meet at a neighbor's house after sundown to organize the hunt. The men would assemble their hunting dogs, some to train with Red, others already good hunting dogs. The men would walk into the woods and release the dogs and then build a small fire and roll tobacco cigarettes (Velvet or Prince Albert) and listen to the dogs. The dogs would take off, eager for the chase. They would scan the forest floor for a scent of another animal. They would track nearly anything, including skunks, raccoons, possums, and squirrels. The men could tell, based upon how the dogs sounded, if they were on a track, or had treed some animal.

When the baying of the dogs changed to their excited barking of treed prey, we would stamp out the fire and head toward the sounds of the dogs.

One afternoon I was walking on the gravel road about a half mile from our Freedom House. I saw a large animal with a very long tail lope across the road and easily jump the fence on the other side. I was sure this was a cougar. I went to Mr. Steven Williams and told him I had seen a wildcat up the road. We spoke with other men who all wanted to see if we could track this animal. We got the dogs together and went to the spot where I had seen the big cat. The dogs caught a scent and were off on the track. We followed for quite some time, stopping occasionally for a rest or cigarettes. Finally we heard the dogs barking treed, and went to the sounds of the excited dogs. The only animal we found in the tree was a possum.

We often exchanged gossip and stories as we sat around a small fire of twigs and dead branches in the woods, as we listened to the hounds. The leaves were like a soft pillow and made sitting in the woods comfortable. We would sit for several minutes or an hour or two. This was an opportunity to tell stories and express opinions. We listened to the sounds of the night, a cacophony of locusts, mosquitos, birds, the swoosh of owls navigating between the trees, and the dogs. There was one flashlight in the group. When we were walking through the woods, we felt safe. The night seemed like a great equalizer. Whomever or whatever we encountered, all life was on an equal footing as there was no discrimination at night in the woods.

The men were open and honest about everything, including their plight as second-class citizens in Mississippi. As a person who had not grown up in a society where I was despised merely for the color of my skin, I was impressed that these men were philosophical about the race issue, and could see an end to racial discrimination and atrocities in Mississippi. These men seemed more open to discussion in the woods than any of them did in their houses or in meetings at their local churches. The only distraction in the woods was the sound of the hounds on track, and that seemed more like music than a distraction.

The local sheriff, the FBI, President Johnson, and President Kennedy were all topics we discussed. National politics seemed more in reach of a solution to racism. Locally, politics was so entrenched that it was difficult to see it changing at all. But nationally, the spirited discussion that led to the passage of the Civil Rights Act of 1964 gave hope to the eventual changing of the guard for local elections in Madison County. Still, it would be another year before the passage of the Voting Rights Act of 1965 that finally made it possible for these men to cast their votes and for their voices to be heard in local elections.

One evening, we were sitting on the front porch of the Freedom House. We saw a rabbit run over by a car in front of our house. I picked up the rabbit, dressed it, and cooked it for supper. The car had fractured some of the bones of the rabbit, and internal organs were squashed. It was a mess, but I cleaned it well. Some volunteers were concerned that eating roadkill was unsanitary. Roadkill, when fresh, is just as good as anything else you can get, especially when you're hungry.

This was a cultural clash between the mostly northern volunteers who were used to going to a local supermarket to buy their food and those of us who were from a culture that valued something to eat, be it from a supermarket, hunting and fishing, or simply found food, as in the case of roadkill. It was also common to harvest wild polk greens and dandelion greens for a salad to go with whatever main course was on the table.

The typical home in Valley View was very much like that of the Williams family. It was a wood frame house with about 600 square feet of living space. It was supported on piers of rocks, bricks, and concrete blocks, about three feet above the ground. Dogs, including Red, Mr. Williams' Redbone hound, pigs, cats, and other animals, all lived under the structure. The single board walls were unpainted on the outside and covered with newspapers on the inside to keep the wind from blowing through the house.

The Williams home in Valley View in 1964.

Mrs. Williams ironing in her home with her walls covered with newspapers to keep out the drafts.

Mrs. Williams in her kitchen in 1964.

The Williams house had electricity and a wood stove for heat in the winter. There was a cooking stove that burned wood and gas with a couple of propane tanks leaning against the outside of the house connected with copper tubing through the wall. This home was divided into sleeping rooms, a kitchen area, a living room, and a porch. The living and visiting took place mainly in the kitchen and on the porch at the front of the house.

The kitchen was composed of a chimney of brick and stone which vented the smoke to the outside of the house. There was no sink, but a washtub in which dirty dishes and pots and pans were placed. There were wooden counters for the preparation of food, and a large kitchen table which was the center of the house for visiting and conversation, as well as eating. Most homes were similar, but many had metal stove pipes from the kitchen through a wall or the roof to take the smoke outside.

There was an outhouse that was periodically moved when the pit beneath became full. There was also a chicken coop, but the chickens were let free to roam during the day, feasting on

Williams boy at home.

insects and whatever plant life managed to survive. The area around the house and adjacent structures was often bare dirt, worn smooth by foot traffic from people and animals, and constantly picked over by the flock of chickens. The chickens went into the fenced coop at night, and were usually shut inside to guard against predators such as skunks and foxes. Even though Mr. Williams had a dog or two, predators still were a problem, as they always seemed to manage to get into the chicken coop while the dogs were sleeping.

Mr. Williams, with whom I went hunting a couple of nights each week, worked picking cotton and working for area farmers. But he also was a preacher, as he "got the calling," as Mrs. Williams explained. He was not the only person in the community to take up preaching, as it was not unknown for a person "to be called by the Lord" to spread the gospel. Mr. Williams did not change much in my estimation, except on Sundays he spent the day telling others how he found Jesus and how he had been called to tell others to turn to Jesus.

Once Phil took a local man, James Sims, a blind musician, to the University Hospital in Jackson, a part of "Ole Miss," the

Mr. James Sims playing his guitar and singing at the Freedom House.

school that had been integrated by James Meredith in 1962. Needless to say, Phil and his black companion were not warmly welcomed on the campus. Upon their return to Canton from Jackson, Phil and Mr. Sims stopped at a black barbershop to get a haircut. Mr. Sims recounted his adventure to the barber, and told him that "My brother stayed right with me the whole time." The barber, knowing Mr. Sims, said, "I didn't know you had a brother." Mr. Sims pointed in Phil's direction and said, "That's my brother sitting right over there." Phil later explained this exchange by stating, "I think that is what we are giving these people this summer, a chance to call a white man brother." Mr. Sims had been blind from birth, and did not have even the vestiges of sight. But a blind black man well understood the segregationist practices of Mississippi.

Mr. Sims carried his guitar on his back in a duffel bag. The guitar was his woman, "Della Mae." He walked with a cane or walking stick that he called his "horse." He was known throughout the county, and was affectionately called "Jimmy Creek," as

Mr. Sims walking, being guided by a child.

he had once walked headlong into a creek as he traversed the county roads on foot. He was good natured about his nickname, but quickly asserted his name, James Sims, when I introduced him to my parents in August of 1964. He played the "Catfish Blues," riffs he had heard and adapted to his style of playing. He was a frequent guest at the Freedom House. He lived in the neighborhood with his girlfriend and was a very social person. He liked to talk about almost any topic and was surprisingly well informed. He was a frequent guest at the homes of others in the community as everyone really enjoyed his singing and playing.

I: The Local White Community

Phil was very focused on the injustice of the society we were challenging on so many fronts. One day we were driving on a gravel road on our way to find a farmer who we were told may be willing to go to the courthouse and try and register to vote. We were rounding a gentle curve when we saw a young black man walking alongside of the road. Phil immediately stopped and asked the passenger to roll down the window. The young man was very wary at being approached by a car full of young white guys and one local black man. He and our black passenger exchanged greetings and tried to establish a rapport. It was shaky at best. Suddenly, a Madison County Sheriff patrol car pulled up behind us with flashing lights. A deputy sheriff exited the patrol car, approached Phil, the driver, and told him he was obstructing traffic and had stopped in the roadway on a curve, which was a traffic offense. Phil tried to argue that he pulled to

Phil driving on a country road with Charles next to him in the car in which they were stopped when Phil received a traffic ticket.

the side of the road to ask the pedestrian if he wanted a ride, and that our cars were the only ones on the road.

I addressed the officer and agreed with him that we had made an ill-advised stop but that there really was no danger to traffic, as our two cars were the only ones we had seen for hours. This particular road was certainly not heavily travelled. He actually smiled, and I felt the tension subside between us. Still, he was unrelenting, but I felt the officer and I had established a rapport.

The officer issued a ticket to Phil, who was fuming. I felt very relieved that we weren't arrested, or that the KKK or the White Citizens' Council did not show up. After the officer left, Phil told me I was siding with the enemy by agreeing with the officer. I felt I had helped defuse a potential deadly encounter. What this illustrates is the extreme stress we all were under on a daily basis in Mississippi. For us as civil rights workers, there was no legal authority we could turn to for assistance in the event of an emergency. And worse, we felt those in authority were the very ones who might harm or murder us.

We had been followed for miles, but we thought the deputy had given up. We were nearly always followed by deputy sheriffs. We had seen the patrol car about half a mile back for some time, but had lost sight of it. We often took circuitous routes to our destinations, including our Freedom School, which was about a mile down the road from our Freedom House. The reason was that if anyone was to follow us, they were in for a long ride. However, it was most likely not at all effective, as all of our activities were very public and often held outside, in plain view from the road.

Life as a civil rights worker was dangerous. There were slugs embedded in the frame of the door in our Freedom House. One night, I observed a line of about fifteen cars go down the dirt road in front of the Freedom House. This was very unusual, because we were in a rural area, at the junction of a dirt road, a gravel road, and an oil and chip road. The only traffic was local and these cars were definitely not owned by local residents. The dirt road was narrow, only room for one car. There were a few homes along the dirt road and near the intersection.

A few minutes later after the cars passed by, I heard a muffled explosion and saw flames leaping into the sky. Shortly thereafter, the line of cars came back on the same route. They drove slowly as if inviting anyone to challenge their presence. The flames were coming from St. John's Baptist Church, a small rural wood frame church nearby. One of the cars, a 1958 Ford, had flashing blinker lights behind the grill. These blinkers were only visible when they were on. I thought I recognized the car as belonging to a former sheriff of Madison County.

St. John's Church was the site of meetings we had organized to encourage people to register and vote, and where we encouraged black farmers and sharecroppers to vote in the upcoming ASCS elections in the fall. It was a wood frame structure with a raised platform in the front of the church and two small rooms to the side of the altar. The following morning after St. John's burned, the FBI came after their Jackson office was called. They arrived just before sunup, about 5: 00 a.m.

St. John's Church in 2014

The FBI agents I spoke with were young, crew cut, polite, and professional. They seemed resigned that they could not find the persons who set the fire, but they were obviously very concerned. We went to the burned-out church. There was nothing left but a foundation, a brick flue, and charred ruins. They took pictures and got our statements. I described the line of cars, the car with the blinkers behind the grill, and the entire incident to them. The FBI took no action that I know of, but they were the only law enforcement agency that I felt I could trust not to retaliate against us.

Later that day, members of the church met at the site of the ruins of their church. I remember speaking to the congregation and telling them that their church was not simply the structure that burned, but St. John's represented their faith and their community which remained intact. I told them that no fire could burn what they believed in and no fire could destroy their community. That day I felt a strong part of that community, because I had shared a local tragedy that affected all of our lives.

That same day, I described the 1958 Ford with the blinkers behind the grill to the Madison County Sheriff. He looked perplexed. I told the Sheriff who I thought the car belonged to, but I never heard anything more about the investigation, if there was one. Today, there is a brick church on the same site, still known as St. John's. It feels good to see the old wooden church has been rebuilt in brick. Now it would be harder to burn.

That same Sheriff would visit the Freedom House often. He would pull into our front yard, closely followed by a line of four or five cars containing deputies. He would ram our front steps with his car and sound his siren to announce his presence. Even though the impact shook our small house, his arrival was not a surprise. We regularly kept watch, 24/7, for vehicles and people approaching our house, and we knew the Sheriff and his deputies were there.

Upon their arrival, the Sheriff and his deputies would just barge into the house through the front door and the back door.

This was very annoying and disconcerting, not to mention a violation of our civil rights under the Fourth Amendment to the U.S. Constitution, for unreasonable search and seizure. Finally, one night I became incensed by this rude and illegal behavior.

One deputy, who I had met on previous visits, jumped out of his car and quickly ran around the house and began to enter the back door of the Freedom House. This deputy was fully armed with a sidearm, a shotgun, a club, and a large flashlight. I met him at the back door and pushed him down the three rickety wooden steps and told him that this was my home and if he wanted to visit, he should knock on the front door. He weakly replied that he was looking for criminals. I told him that there were no criminals here and he knew it. He meekly went around to the front door.

In retrospect, I could have been shot and killed that night for assaulting a police officer. It was my luck that the deputy was chagrined at his own despicable behavior and did not challenge me. At the time, I was twenty years old, wearing cut off jeans, no shirt, and flip flops. I probably weighed 140 pounds. I was hardly in any position to pose a threat to anyone, certainly not a deputy sheriff in uniform, fully armed. Phil followed me to the back of the house and witnessed the entire episode. He said he wanted to see what I was doing.

One evening about sundown, several of the volunteers were sitting on the steps of the Freedom House. A pickup truck slowly drove by on the road in front of the house. One of the persons in the Freedom House noticed flames from a fire burning in the back of the pickup truck. We all started waving and shouting at the truck to alert them to the fire, but it accelerated away down the road. Some of the civil rights workers jumped into a car and sped off toward the pickup truck to warn them of the fire in their vehicle.

After a minute or two, a ball of fire rose in the evening sky about one half mile away, on the road from the direction of the pickup truck and the car of civil rights workers. Carolyn and I ran along the fence row looking for the car in which the other civil rights workers were riding. We tried to remain hidden from view by the foliage, and we ran in a crouched position. We were very relieved to find that there was no damage to the car in which our colleagues were riding.

In fact, one of our colleagues told me that when they got close to the truck, someone in the back of the truck threw a bottle of gasoline in which a lighted wick was burning. This Molotov cocktail landed harmlessly on the road. It is ironic that we were trying to help the people in the truck, whereas they were trying to harm or kill us. This is but one example of the irony of being a civil rights worker in 1964 in Mississippi.

We were idealistic and thought we were going to help everyone. However, many people did not see us in that light. We were seen by many in the white community as "outside agitators" bent on their destruction. Their violent reaction to our presence was testament to their fears. The perception from the black community was very different, however. We were seen as helping erase centuries of discrimination. Our role in the black community was multifaceted.

One of our roles was to educate the adults in the black community as to their civil rights. This included educating them about their right to vote, and encouraging them to try to register to vote in the county courthouse. Of course, they all knew the dangers of trying to register to vote much better than we did. In every home I visited, there were almost always two pictures on the wall: That of John F. Kennedy, and that of Abraham Lincoln. Each man represented a step forward in the quest for freedom in the lives of the members of the black community. Lincoln was revered because of the Emancipation Proclamation, and Kennedy was likewise revered because he had proposed the passage of the Civil Rights Act. The Civil Rights Act was passed during the summer of 1964, but it had little effect on the daily lives of black citizens in Mississippi.

Andy Greene and I became close friends as well as co-directors of the Valley View project. In the fall, we met daily and I visited with him and his adopted family often. I was visiting there during Thanksgiving and there was a television program with holiday music and entertainment. One of the performers was Nat King Cole. When Mr. Cole began to sing, the local television station blocked out the audio portion of the broadcast with loud static. This interruption lasted until the last note died from Mr. Cole's lips. It was blatant censorship of a black performer. Andy and his family just shook their heads and sighed. This is just another example of the racism that was expressed in every aspect of life in Mississippi in 1964.

Charles when he and Carolyn handed out flyers to farmers and sharecroppers.

Civil rights volunteers meet on the porch of a sharecropper.

James Sims.

Mr. Sims walking on a country road to the Freedom House.

Charles driving car with other volunteers canvassing for voters.

Children singing at Freedom School.

A country store where we canvassed for voters.

A group meeting where a volunteer played a guitar.

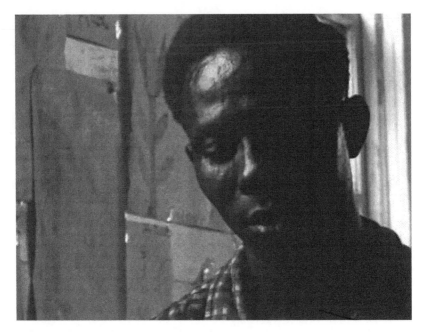

A local man learning to read at the Freedom School.

A meeting under a tree with volunteers and local residents.

Volunteers encourage men at a country store to register and vote.

Local women do their wash outside in their yard.

Richard Beymer

Meeting under the shade of a tree.

3

Selma-Montgomery March

I worked on the Selma-Montgomery March from Selma, Alabama, to Montgomery, Alabama, in the spring of 1965. This historic march began on March 7, 1965, with "Bloody Sunday," the day of the first attempt of the people of Selma to march to their state capitol in Montgomery and to deliver a list of grievances to their governor, George Wallace. A second attempt was made on March 9, but when the troopers stepped aside at the Pettus Bridge, Dr. King led the marchers back to a church. After this futile attempt, the final thrust was on March 21, 1965. The march was successful and reached Montgomery where the marchers delivered their list to the state capitol.

The purpose of the march is enshrined in the First Amendment to our Constitution: "Congress shall make no law respecting an establishment of religion, or prohibiting the free exercise thereof; or abridging the freedom of speech, or of the press; or the right of the people peaceably to assemble, and to petition the Government for a redress of grievances." The people of Selma wanted to march to Montgomery and petition their governor to address many grievances confronting them as citizens of the State of Alabama.

On March 15, 1965, President Johnson addressed the Congress, identifying himself with the demonstrators in Selma in a televised address: "Their cause must be our cause too. Because it is not just Negroes, but really it is all of us, who must overcome the crippling legacy of bigotry and injustice. And we shall overcome" (Johnson, "Special Message"). The following day Selma demonstrators submitted a detailed march plan to federal Judge Frank M. Johnson, Jr., who approved the demonstration and enjoined Governor Wallace and local law enforcement from harassing or threatening the marchers. On March 17, President Johnson submitted the Voting Rights Act legislation to Congress.

Frank M. Johnson, Jr. was a federal jurist from Alabama. He ordered the State of Alabama to allow the march from Selma to Montgomery. He issued the order only after getting the assurance of President Lyndon Johnson that it would be enforced. Because of the controversy surrounding the cases and intense opposition to change, federal marshals provided him round-the-clock protection for almost fifteen years, beginning after a cross was burned on the lawn in front of his house, and the bombing of his mother's home in the mistaken belief that the home was his.

Judge Johnson held, in *Williams vs. Wallace*, 240 F. Supp. 100, 106-07 (M.D. Ala. 1965), "This Court has the duty and responsibility in this case of drawing the "constitutional boundary line." In doing so, it seems basic to our constitutional principles that the extent of the right to assemble, demonstrate and march peaceably along the highways and streets in an orderly manner should be commensurate with the enormity of the wrongs that are being protested and petitioned against. In this case, the wrongs are enormous. The extent of the right to demonstrate against these wrongs should be determined accordingly. This is true even though it is recognized that the right to exercise constitutional rights by marching alongside a public highway must be narrowed in the sense that such a right is subject to greater regulation and in the sense that greater abridgment of the right may, depending upon the circumstances, be

warranted.... The proclamation as issued by the Governor of
the State of Alabama on March 6, 1965, absolutely banning any
march by any manner-regardless of how conducted-and stating
that such a march will not be tolerated, constituted an unreasonable interference with the right of Negro citizens engaged
in the march to use U.S. Highway 80 in the manner they were
seeking to use it on Sunday, March 7, 1965. Such a proclamation by the Governor of the State of Alabama, as enforced by
the Alabama State Troopers and deputies and "possemen" of
Dallas County, Alabama, stepped across the "constitutional
boundary line" that lies between the interests of the public to
use the highway in general and the right of American citizens
to use it for the purpose of marching to the seat of their State
government-Montgomery, Alabama-for the purpose of protesting their grievances.'"

We worked night and day planning the march. We divided
the volunteers up into work parties. Some people cooked, and
some learned how to put up tents. Others secured porta potties
and other needed supplies. We stockpiled ponchos, water jugs,
clothing, blankets, and just about anything that we thought
might be needed on the march.

I was in a planning meeting one morning at a local church,
when in walked Rev. Hosea Williams, one of Rev. Dr. Martin
Luther King's organizers. With him were a young couple who
had apparently just donated money to our cause. Rev. Williams
got everyone to sing some freedom songs in honor of the couple
who were supporting our cause. After we told Rev. Williams
that we were making progress and we would appreciate it if he
would let us continue our work, he left with the young couple.

In Selma, my hometown buddy Chuck Neblett and I were
talking on a street near the Brown Chapel. Chuck is one of the
original Freedom Singers, and a long-time civil rights activist. He has scars on his head from a beating he received as he
escaped from a KKK rally. Chuck had donned a white sheet and
walked into the rally. His black hands gave him away, and as he

Brown Chapel in Selma, Alabama.

scrambled over a fence in a fast retreat, he was pummeled by screaming KKK members brandishing folding metal chairs. He still retained that invincible mindset in Selma. He and I were discussing how to put "We Shall Overcome: SNCC" bumper stickers on all the Selma police cruisers. Then Chuck said, "Do you want to meet Martin?"

Dr. King was coming down some stairs nearby, and said, "Hi, Chuck." Chuck approached him and said, "Martin, this is Charles, from my hometown." His presence was warm and inviting, and he was introduced as "Martin," not the Rev. Dr. Martin Luther King, Jr., winner of the Nobel Peace Prize. He asked me what I had been doing in the civil rights movement. For the next several minutes, Martin, Chuck, and I stood in the street as I recounted our work for the Mississippi Freedom Summer. I told Dr. King how we organized and ran Freedom Schools and our strategies to register people to vote, including helping to organize the Mississippi Freedom Democratic Party.

In our conversation, I highlighted our work for the black farmers of Madison County. I explained that sixty percent of the farmland was owned by black farmers, but they had no say in farming policies through federal programs administered by the U.S. Department of Agriculture because they had no representation on the governing boards that decided who received crop allotments and other federal subsidies. I told Dr. King how we organized meetings in black churches in rural Madison County. The federal government did not practice racial segregation in the voting process, as did the State of Mississippi, so voting was less of a problem. There had never been any black representative on this board since Reconstruction. The Valley View Project in December of 1964 elected black farmers as their representatives on the governing board.

Dr. King listened to my stories with interest. He kept plying me with questions. He was interested in our strategies, especially in what worked and what didn't. He was very humble and put me completely at ease speaking with him. I was impressed that he wanted to hear from me, a twenty year old college student, and was so attentive to the details of our campaign on behalf of the black farmers. I felt honored I had met and spoken with Dr. King the person, as well as the national icon of the civil rights movement.

The atmosphere in Selma was far different from my experiences in Mississippi. The Selma police knew they were outnumbered. Chuck and I crawled up to several police cruisers and placed bumper stickers on them proclaiming "We Shall Overcome: SNCC." We proudly watched them drive around town proclaiming support for the civil rights movement. If they saw us, they never said anything.

The Selma Police Department really kept to themselves and away from the churches and meetings that preceded the march. It seemed that they were under orders to leave everyone alone and not interfere with the march in any way. Their behavior was so different from the police I encountered in Mississippi the year before, who were always in your face, claiming the turf as their own. It was somewhat refreshing to be able to walk down the streets in Selma and not be challenged by the police simply for being there.

Selma was fine as long as you remained on the black side of town. We ventured out of town to scope out possible places for the marchers to camp on their way to Montgomery. As soon as we crossed the Pettus Bridge over the Alabama River, we began to encounter the local racists who had already twice prevented this march from taking place. White men in pickup trucks, with their guns on the racks, drove slowly by. Others appeared on horseback toting guns. At that time, we were without the protection of the nationalized Alabama National Guard. We felt very vulnerable, as we believed these people were the same ones who had previously thwarted the march. At least there were no police among the people who were trying to intimidate us, as there had been on previous occasions. Fortunately, we were not physically harassed or beaten.

Most of the volunteers had their meals at local churches that provided free food for the organizers who spent weeks of planning and preparations for the march. These churches continued to provide sustenance for the volunteers, as most did not actually march but were support staff for the marchers. But some did venture into the main part of town which was all white. Some people were able to get served at local restaurants, but most did not even test the equal opportunity that was theoretically available to everyone in businesses that were engaged in public accommodations or interstate commerce, or both.

The influx of people from all around the country nearly overwhelmed the small town of Selma. The streets were filled with cars with out of state license plates. One of the most common was New York. Everyone found a place to stay. I slept on a bare wooden floor in my sleeping bag. Next to me was an actor from New York, Gary Merrill, who had driven from New York to Selma in his Mercedes 450 SL. Gary was fairly typical of the

Marchers cross the Edmond Pettus Bridge in Selma, 1965.

volunteers who came to Selma. He was on the crew that erected the tents in which the marchers slept during the march. He worked hard and was glad to be a part of this historical event, although at the time, we did not know it would become one of the more famous demonstrations for civil rights our county has ever seen. It seems very ironic that it took the National Guard to protect people who just wanted to express their constitutional rights by marching on a public road to their state capitol to present their governor with a list of grievances, as specified in the First Amendment.

One morning, I was walking to Brown Chapel for an organizational meeting. A couple of blocks in front of me, I saw a large group of people clustered at a fence. When I got closer, I saw a young boy about fourteen years old plowing a half acre field. He was using a mule, something that apparently no one next to the fence had ever seen. I saw at least fifty cameras taking pictures of this apparent spectacle. The young boy was incredulous. He wondered what the fuss was all about, as he had been plowing this field and others with this mule for a few years, just like his father. This is but one clash of cultures that was apparent in Selma that spring.

Most of the visitors were also volunteers helping organize the march. I drove the press car, but at first, every member of the press wanted to walk with the marchers. At the beginning of the march, I parked the press car and walked across the Pettus Bridge with Dr. King and the rest of the marchers. Then I drove slowly behind the main body of marchers to the first campsite.

I left Selma during the second day of the March. My sister Kay and I were enrolled for the spring semester at SIU, and classes were starting the following day. The three days of the march were punctuated by a large rally on the third evening at a campsite, and by a large rally in downtown Montgomery attended by over 25,000 people.

Attending this march had a profound effect on me, as it did on our nation. For the first time, I saw a diverse cross section of our citizenry shed their economic, cultural, social, and educational differences and come together in an environment that was hostile. This was not the capitol mall in Washington, D.C. This was Selma, Alabama, where just a few days before, marchers had been beaten bloody for trying to march across the Pettus Bridge. In Selma, there was a history and a real threat of violence to anyone who dared challenge the Jim Crow mentality. But these threats were not a deterrence. People from all around our country came and put themselves and their lives on the line. The momentum that began at lunch counters, in the bus stations, and on the capitol mall, became an irresistible force that is still forcing changes in our society today.

4

Years Later

I have often returned to Mississippi and my friends in Valley View. For years it was an annual trip, then on holidays. Each time the changes were a very welcome reminder of the work we had accomplished at organizing the community. Our community was now self-sustaining politically, socially, economically, and educationally. Local leaders took control of all of these venues and the changes were dramatic.

In 1994, I attended the thirtieth reunion of the Mississippi Freedom Summer held at Tougaloo College. It was a welcome reunion for many, including myself. Chuck Neblett was there, as well as his brother Chico Neblett (Seku Neblett). Both brothers were civil rights activists and Student Nonviolent Coordinating Committee members.

The organizers had vans for volunteers and staff to visit our old haunts. As I traveled through rural Mississippi on my way to Valley View and Canton, we rounded a curve and a pickup truck was coming the other way. There were two young white men in the truck with their rifles and shotguns proudly displayed behind them in a gun rack. I promptly hit the deck, trying to shield myself from them and their retaliation. Of course there was none. I was reacting as I had done many times in 1964, when such an encounter could lead to violence and gunfire. I realized I had been battling Post Traumatic Stress

Disorder (PTSD) for many years.

A little further on, we pulled into a small convenience store. While we were there, a pickup truck pulling a horse trailer, driven by a black driver with black passengers, pulled in, and next to it another truck filled with white guys parked very close. The black guys got out and reached into the back of their truck. They lifted out two six packs of beer, and began throwing them to the passengers in the other truck. They knew each other, and were friends.

As we continued retracing our path from 1964, we drove into Greenwood, Mississippi. When we arrived at the courthouse, a clerk met our van and told us the Sheriff wanted to see us. My stomach dropped, because in 1964, we were subject to arrest simply for being on the courthouse square. After a few minutes, the Sheriff appeared. He was black, and he gave us the keys to the city!

One of the largest landowners in Madison County in 1964 was Rev. McCullough. He was retired when I met him, as he rode around the country roads and fields on his little black mare. He wore a large brimmed straw hat, bib overalls, and was welcomed everywhere. He had a large family and was the patriarch of his clan. His sons were community leaders as well.

One of his many children, Jessie McCullough, owned the Valley View Freedom House where many of the civil rights workers lived, including me. Mr. Jessie McCullough was not able to vote in 1964, but he did register after the Voting Rights Act was passed in 1965. When I returned for a visit in 1994, Mr. McCullough was a Madison County Supervisor. He was an elected public official, driving a Madison County car. This was a great improvement to his having to endure being called "boy" by the local whites, which I observed in 1964.

When the schools were finally desegregated in Mississippi, public education suffered. For example, in Madison County Mississippi, all white high school students went to a Christian school. When the Christian school was established, they removed much of the equipment and supplies from the public school. After a long legal battle, the equipment was returned. However, it was not returned in the condition in which it was taken. For example, the lights to the athletic field at the high school had been removed and taken to the Christian school. When those lights were returned, they were unceremoniously dumped in the middle of the football field. They were not erected nor were they hooked up.

In 2004, Richard Beymer and I traveled to Mississippi in order to interview some of the people in his original movie, "A Regular Bouquet." This was a very successful trip, and we managed to contact many people whom we filmed in 1964. I show "A Regular Bouquet" about a dozen times each year to groups and history students at local colleges and schools.

During the summer of 1964, many black persons were encouraged to run for public office. One such person approached a local television station in Jackson, Mississippi, for advertising time for his campaign. The staff of the station rejected his advertising, telling him in stark language that they "would never sell advertising to a nigger." I met him thirty years later, when he recounted this story. By then, he was the CEO of that very television station.

The Valley View Community Center on Otha Williams land, 50 years later.

Robert Chinn presented certificates of appreciation to civil rights workers in 2014.

Mr. Otha Williams, our neighbor at the Valley View Freedom House, donated a portion of his cotton field to build a community center.

After the violence had subsided, the American Friends Service Committee, a Quaker organization, built a cinder block building, complete with a commercial kitchen, on the site across the road from the Freedom House. This was used for job training, child care, and community meetings. This structure was built because of the strong community involvement from the families in the Valley View area.

There are many stories of people who were involved in the civil rights struggle in 1964 that should be told. One of those is of the Chinn family who hosted a reception in our honor in 2004. This family consisted of Mr. C.O. Chinn, his wife and children, one of whom was Robert Chinn, known as "Junior." Robert was as fearless as his father.

Eating out was a rare treat, and C.O. Chinn, another fearless

The Canton Freedom House, now a civil rights museum.

local entrepreneur, provided the cuisine and a safe environment. Chinn's Restaurant was the only place an integrated group could be served a meal in Canton. We visited Chinn's when we could afford it.

Mr. Chinn was rumored to be a moonshiner and drove fast cars to outrun law enforcement officials. On one occasion, Mr. Chinn, Phil, and Bill were returning from Jackson. Mr. Chinn stopped for gas and the attendant told him a lug nut was loose on a front wheel. The attendant graciously offered to tighten it for him. A few miles later, as they drove into Canton, the wheel came off the car. Fortunately, no one was hurt and the car was not damaged. Mr. Chinn laughed about it, but he was wary of ever letting anyone do anything to his car without observing what they were doing.

Mr. Chinn had a son, Robert, who was married to Mamie, and they had daughters. In 1964, black citizens who wanted to register to vote took their lives in their hands when they went in the courthouse. At the courthouse, they could have been charged with trespassing on public property, or carrying a sign. After passage of the Voting Rights Act of 1965 and the registration of hundreds of black voters in Madison County, Robert and Mamie Chinn both were elected judges in Madison County, Mississippi.

The changes that resulted from the Voting Rights Act of 1965 were far reaching. When it became possible to register to vote, a majority of black citizens in Mississippi registered and voted. This was possible only because the federal examiners monitored the voter registration process and insured that it was being conducted in a fair and responsible manner.

One of most dramatic changes was the election of black public officials in Mississippi. Fifty years after the Mississippi Freedom Summer, Mississippi has the largest number of black public officials per capita in the nation. This affected all governmental services. There were blacks elected as sheriffs, county supervisors, judges, school board members, and many more public offices. This in itself was a long awaited result of the registration of black voters.

As part of the 50th reunion of the Mississippi Freedom Summer held at Tougaloo College in Jackson, Mississippi, in June of 2014, I attended a reception held in Canton, Mississippi, for the civil rights workers from 1964. We were given certificates of appreciation by the Canton City Council, who wanted to jail us in 1964. We also received Mississippi State Senate Concurrent Resolution No. 589 thanking us for our work in 1964. Even though we were happy to receive these awards, they showed us the irony of the passage of time, as both bodies wanted us gone 50 years ago.

At the Canton reception, I met a woman, Vickie Mc Neill, who had been fourteen years old in 1964, and a Freedom School student. Vickie saw how we were being treated by the Canton police, so she told her mother and us that she wanted to be a police officer. Her mother told her to forget about it, but we told her she could do anything she wanted. In 1978, she became the

Vickie Mc Neill

first black female police officer in Canton. In 2008, she became the first black female Chief of Police in Canton, and one of the first in Mississippi.

Life in Mississippi and all across the South was changed forever. Segregation still exists in the hearts and minds of many white southerners, but now persons of color have the state and federal courts on their side. And local law enforcement as well as the justice system and the educational system are no longer totally white. But the recent Supreme Court decision striking down a key part of the 1965 Voting Rights Act has given rise to the same issues surrounding voting. State legislatures in the South have enacted legislation to limit the right to vote. They have targeted the same population that was protected from discrimination in 1965. This fight for freedom and universal suffrage is far from over.

Otha Williams, Jr., a Freedom School student in 1964, is the son of Otha Williams, who was a fearless community leader during the civil rights struggle. As our nearest neighbor, Mr. Williams became one of our most trusted friends in 1964. He

Otha Williams, Jr. and Charles in Valley View in 2014.

had a history of conflicts with the local sheriff and spent time in jail on a trumped up charge, but he was so resilient and had such a powerful personality that none of that seemed to phase him at all. He always kept his sense of humor and his focus on attaining his rights as a U.S. citizen, especially the right to vote.

The experiences I had in Mississippi in 1964 cemented in me the resolve to lead a nonviolent life based on the example of Gandhi. I became a conscientious objector to the draft and served our society in a civilian capacity at the University of Chicago Hospitals and Clinics.

These certificates from the City of Canton and the State of Mississippi were presented to civil rights workers fifty years after the Mississippi Freedom Summer.

SENATE CONCURRENT RESOLUTION NO. 589

A CONCURRENT RESOLUTION TO COMMEMORATE THE 50TH ANNIVERSARY OF THE FREEDOM SUMMER OF 1964 CIVIL RIGHTS MOVEMENT IN MISSISSIPPI, TO RECOGNIZE THE SOCIAL CONTRIBUTIONS OF THESE VOLUNTEERS AND TO WELCOME THE "MISSISSIPPI FREEDOM SUMMER 50TH ANNIVERSARY CONFERENCE" TO OUR STATE.

WHEREAS, "Freedom Summer" was a campaign in Mississippi to register African-American voters during the summer of 1964. In the summer of 1964, more than 1,000 summer volunteers from across America convened in Mississippi to put an end to the system of rigid segregation. The Civil Rights workers and the summer volunteers successfully challenged the denial by the State of Mississippi to keep blacks from voting, getting a decent education, and holding elected offices; and

WHEREAS, as a result of the Freedom Summer of 1964, some of the barriers to voting have been eliminated and Mississippi has close to 1,000 black state and local elected officials. In fact, Mississippi has more black elected officials than any other state in the union. While the Freedom Summer of 1964 made profound changes in the State of Mississippi and the country, much remains to be accomplished; and

WHEREAS, this voting rights initiative was led by the Student Nonviolent Coordinating Committee (SNCC), with the support of the Council of Federated Organizations (COFO), which included the National Association for the Advancement of Colored People (NAACP), the Congress of Racial Equality (CORE), and the Southern Christian Leadership Conference (SCLC); and

WHEREAS, thousands of students and activists participated in two-week orientation sessions in preparation for the voter registration drive in Mississippi. Three Civil Rights volunteers lost their lives in their attempts to secure voting rights for blacks. The national uproar in response to these brave men's deaths helped raise the political capital necessary to bring about passage of the Voting Rights Act of 1965; and

WHEREAS, the Mississippi Freedom Summer 50th Anniversary Conference will convene in Jackson, Mississippi, on June 25-29, 2014, both to recognize the accomplishments and those who worked for changes to the politically segregated Mississippi and to discuss how to continue the effort toward Mississippi reaching its full potential for all of its citizens; and

WHEREAS, "While this 50th Anniversary will highlight the legacy of the Freedom Summer accomplishments, it will also serve as the platform to continue to make life better for Jacksonians, Mississippians and all Americans," said the late Jackson Mayor Chowke Lumumba. "This is a remarkable occasion. As we remember Nelson Mandela, this is a reminder of the sacrifices of our own homegrown freedom fighters. This will be a world renowned showcasing of the contribution to move the world forward. This is a legacy, a living treasure, not a buried one"; and

WHEREAS, we note the historical context and significance of this event and these Mississippi Civil Rights Pioneers who ignited the consciousness of America to its responsibilities:

NOW, THEREFORE, BE IT RESOLVED BY THE SENATE OF THE STATE OF MISSISSIPPI, THE HOUSE OF REPRESENTATIVES CONCURRING THEREIN, That we do hereby commemorate the 50th Anniversary of the Freedom Summer of 1964 Civil Rights Movement in Mississippi, recognize the social contributions of these volunteers who came to our state and extend the welcome of the Legislature to the "Mississippi Freedom Summer 50th Anniversary Conference" to be held in Jackson on June 25-29, 2014, to remember the contributions of these Pioneers of the Civil Rights Movement in our country.

BE IT FURTHER RESOLVED, That this resolution be presented to the Chairman of the Mississippi Freedom Summer 50th Anniversary Conference, and the following Freedom Summer Volunteers: Mr. Charney Bromberg, Mr. Phillip Sharpe, Ms. Jo Ann Robinson, Mr. Charles Pickette, Mr. Peter Pretz, Mr. Thom Manoff, Mr. William Forsythe, Mrs. Myrtis Raymond and Reverend Rims Barber.

ADOPTED BY THE SENATE
March 4, 2014

ADOPTED BY THE HOUSE OF REPRESENTATIVES
March 18, 2014

LIEUTENANT GOVERNOR TATE REEVES
PRESIDENT OF THE SENATE

PHILIP GUNN
SPEAKER OF THE HOUSE OF REPRESENTATIVES

SENATOR KENNETH WAYNE JONES, DISTRICT 21

Acknowledgements

There are many images and quotes in this book from Richard Beymer's "A Regular Bouquet" and outtakes from the footage shot in 1964. There are several pictures of me building the outhouse and taking a shower in the shower I made from a five gallon lard can. There are images of our Freedom School, our Freedom House, students, both children and adults, and families with children picking cotton. I was present at most of the filming and recording of the narrations by my fellow civil rights workers. I was the cameraman in the scenes in the cane field, that of Richard chopping cane to be fed through the crusher to make molasses, and Richard and a child sharing the sweet pulp of a cane stalk. The movie, "A Regular Bouquet," may be viewed at: https://wufilmarchive.wordpress.com/2014/10/31/a-regular-bouquet-mississippi-summer.

Other images were taken by Charles Prickett, Otha Williams, Jr., and Glen Cotton. Images not from these sources include:

1. Cooling feet in the reflecting pool at the March on Washington: Leffler, Warren K., photographer, in the Library of Congress: http://commons.wikimedia.org/wiki/File:Demonstrators_sit,_with_their_feet_in_the_Reflecting_Pool,_during_the_March_on_Washington.jpg.

2. Fannie Lou Hamer: Herbert Bobs Tusa, photograper. *Faces of Freedom Summer.* Tuscaloosa: University Alabama Press, 2001; Freedom Summer Digital Collection, www.wisconsinhistory.org.

3. Newspaper article of firebombing in Canton: http: //search.freedomarchives.org/search.php?s=bomb#.

4. Newspaper article showing candidates for the Mississippi Freedom Democratic Party: http://search.freedomarchives.org/search.php?s=candidates+# .

5. Dr. King speaking at the March on Washington: www.loc.gov/exhibits/march-on-washington/bob-adelman.html.

6. The differences in the prepared and delivered speech by John Lewis can be found at billmoyers.com.

7. The "I Have A Dream" speech by Martin Luther King, Jr. is reprinted by permission, Writers House LLC.

8. The image of the Edmund Pettus Bridge and marchers is from NBC News and obtained from public domain images, Google.

9. The image of Brown Chapel, Selma: www.thedriveabout.blogspot.com.

10. The picture of Charles on the back cover was taken by Christopher Chung and is printed by permission of the *Press Democrat* newspaper in Santa Rosa, California.

11. The Horace Doyle Barnette declaration is found at www.law2.umkc.edu.

12. Appendices III (literacy tests), IV (MFDP-COFO), and V (ASCS-COFO) are all from www.crmvet.org.

I owe appreciation to Brian Kaapcke for urging me to recall and write these accounts of my experiences in the civil rights movement. I thank my wife Susan Eschler for her support and editing of this manuscript, as well as Emerson Stafford, Janet Stafford, my sister Kay Michener, Carol Tewes, Carol Grzelak, Janis Bellinger, Tiffany Weaver, Megan Rhodes, Allison Baker, Ashley Atkins, Jennifer Talak, Chuck Miller, and Richard Tewes. My friend Bob Presley did the cover collage. Special thanks to Jo-Anne Rosen, my publisher, who was very thorough and patient with every version of this book.

APPENDICES

Appendix I

Appendix I is the Reverend Dr. Martin Luther King, Jr.'s August 28, 1963, "I Have a Dream" speech.

I Have a Dream

I am happy to join with you today in what will go down in history as the greatest demonstration for freedom in the history of our nation.

Five score years ago, a great American, in whose symbolic shadow we stand today, signed the Emancipation Proclamation. This momentous decree came as a great beacon light of hope to millions of Negro slaves who had been seared in the flames of withering injustice. It came as a joyous daybreak to end the long night of their captivity.

But one hundred years later, the Negro still is not free. One hundred years later, the life of the Negro is still sadly crippled by the manacles of segregation and the chains of discrimination. One hundred years later, the Negro lives on a lonely island of poverty in the midst of a vast ocean of material prosperity. One hundred years later, the Negro is still languished in the corners of American society and finds himself an exile in his own land. And so we've come here today to dramatize a shameful condition.

In a sense we've come to our nation's capital to cash a check. When the architects of our republic wrote the magnificent words of the Constitution and the Declaration of Independence, they were signing a promissory note to which every American was to fall heir. This note was a promise that all men, yes, black men as well as white men, would be guaranteed the "unalienable Rights" of "Life, Liberty and the pursuit of Happiness." It is obvious today that America has defaulted on this promissory note, insofar as her citizens of color are concerned. Instead of honoring this sacred obligation, America has given the Negro people a bad check, a check which has come back marked "insufficient funds."

But we refuse to believe that the bank of justice is bankrupt. We refuse to believe that there are insufficient funds in the great vaults of opportunity of this nation. And so, we've come to cash this check, a check that will give us upon demand the riches of freedom and the security of justice.

We have also come to this hallowed spot to remind America of the fierce urgency of Now. This is no time to engage in the luxury of cooling off or to take the tranquilizing drug of gradualism. Now is the time to make real the promises of democracy. Now is the time to rise from the dark and desolate valley of segregation to the sunlit path of racial justice. Now is the time to lift our nation from the quicksands of racial injustice to the solid rock of brotherhood. Now is the time to make justice a reality for all of God's children.

It would be fatal for the nation to overlook the urgency of the moment. This sweltering summer of the Negro's legitimate discontent will not pass until there is an invigorating autumn of freedom and equality. Nineteen sixty-three is not an end, but a beginning. And those who hope that the Negro needed to blow off steam and will now be content will have a rude awakening if the nation returns to business as usual. And there will be neither rest nor tranquility in America until the Negro is granted his citizenship rights. The whirlwinds of revolt will continue to shake the foundations of our nation until the bright day of justice emerges.

But there is something that I must say to my people, who stand on the warm threshold which leads into the palace of justice: In the process of gaining our rightful place, we must not be guilty of wrongful deeds. Let us not seek to satisfy our thirst for freedom by drinking from the cup of bitterness and hatred. We must forever conduct our struggle on the high plane of dignity and discipline. We must not allow our creative protest to degenerate into physical violence. Again and again, we must rise to the majestic heights of meeting physical force with soul force.

The marvelous new militancy which has engulfed the Negro community must not lead us to a distrust of all white people, for many of our white brothers, as evidenced by their presence here today, have come to realize that their destiny is tied up with our destiny. And they have come to realize that their freedom is inextricably bound to our freedom.

We cannot walk alone.

And as we walk, we must make the pledge that we shall always march ahead.

We cannot turn back.

There are those who are asking the devotees of civil rights, "When will you be satisfied?" We can never be satisfied as long as the Negro is the victim of the unspeakable horrors of police brutality. We can never be satisfied as long as our bodies, heavy with the fatigue of travel, cannot gain lodging in the motels of the highways and the hotels of the cities. We cannot be satisfied as long as the negro's basic mobility is from a smaller ghetto to a larger one. We can never be satisfied as long as our children are stripped of their self-hood and robbed of their dignity by signs stating: "For Whites Only." We cannot be satisfied as long as a Negro in Mississippi cannot vote and a Negro in New York believes he has nothing for which to vote. No, no, we are not satisfied, and we will not be satisfied until "justice rolls down like waters, and righteousness like a mighty stream."

I am not unmindful that some of you have come here out of great trials and tribulations. Some of you have come fresh from narrow jail cells. And some of you have come from areas where your quest — quest for freedom left you battered by the storms of persecution and staggered by the winds of police brutality. You have been the veterans of creative suffering. Continue to work with the faith that unearned suffering is redemptive. Go back to Mississippi, go back to Alabama, go back to South Carolina, go back to Georgia, go back to Louisiana, go back to the slums and ghettos of our northern cities, knowing that somehow this situation can and will be changed.

Let us not wallow in the valley of despair, I say to you today, my friends.

And so even though we face the difficulties of today and tomorrow, I still have a dream. It is a dream deeply rooted in the American dream.

I have a dream that one day this nation will rise up and live out the true meaning of its creed: "We hold these truths to be self-evident, that all men are created equal."

I have a dream that one day on the red hills of Georgia, the sons of former slaves and the sons of former slave owners will be able to sit down together at the table of brotherhood.

I have a dream that one day even the state of Mississippi, a state sweltering with the heat of injustice, sweltering with the heat of oppression, will be transformed into an oasis of freedom and justice.

I have a dream that my four little children will one day live in a nation where they will not be judged by the color of their skin but by the content of their character.

I have a *dream* today!

I have a dream that one day, down in Alabama, with its vicious racists, with its governor having his lips dripping with the words of "interposition" and "nullification" — one day right there in Alabama little black boys and black girls will be able to join hands with little white boys and white girls as sisters and brothers.

I have a *dream* today!

I have a dream that one day every valley shall be exalted, and every hill and mountain shall be made low, the rough places will be made plain, and the crooked places will be made straight; "and the glory of the Lord shall be revealed and all flesh shall see it together."

This is our hope, and this is the faith that I go back to the South with.

With this faith, we will be able to hew out of the mountain of despair a stone of hope. With this faith, we will be able to transform the jangling discords of our nation into a beautiful symphony of brotherhood. With this faith, we will be able to work together, to pray together, to struggle together, to go to jail together, to stand up for freedom together, knowing that we will be free one day.

And this will be the day — this will be the day when all of God's children will be able to sing with new meaning:

My country 'tis of thee, sweet land of liberty, of thee I sing.
Land where my fathers died, land of the Pilgrim's pride,
From every mountainside, let freedom ring!

And if America is to be a great nation, this must become true.

And so let freedom ring from the prodigious hilltops of New Hampshire.

Let freedom ring from the mighty mountains of New York.

Let freedom ring from the heightening Alleghenies of Pennsylvania.

Let freedom ring from the snow-capped Rockies of Colorado.

Let freedom ring from the curvaceous slopes of California.

But not only that:

Let freedom ring from Stone Mountain of Georgia.

Let freedom ring from Lookout Mountain of Tennessee.

Let freedom ring from every hill and molehill of Mississippi.

From every mountainside, let freedom ring.

And when this happens, and when we allow freedom ring, when we let it ring from every village and every hamlet, from every state and every city, we will be able to speed up that day when all of God's children, black men and white men, Jews and Gentiles, Protestants and Catholics, will be able to join hands and sing in the words of the old Negro spiritual:

Free at last! Free at last!
Thank God Almighty, we are free at last!

Appendix II

Appendix II is the declaration of Horace D. Barnette, who witnessed and participated in the murders of James Chaney, Michael Schwerner, and Andy Goodman.

CONFESSION OF HORACE DOYLE BARNETTE
NOVEMBER 20, 1964

Horace Doyle Barnette's Nov. 20, 1964, confession to the FBI

From FBI documents

FEDERAL BUREAU OF INVESTIGATION

Date: 11/24/64

The following is a signed statement which was furnished by HORACE DOYLE BARNETTE on November 20, 1964:

Springhill, La.

Nov. 20, 1964

"I, Horace Doyle Barnette, do hereby make this free and voluntary statement to Special Agent Henry Rask and Special Agent James A. Wooten, who have identified themselves to me to be special agents of the Federal Bureau of Investigation and Special Agent Henry Rask have informed me that I do not have to make a statement, that any statement made by me can be used against me in a court of law and that I am entitled to consult with an attorney before making this statement and that if I can not afford an attorney and I am required to appear in court, the court will appoint one for me. That no force, threats or promises were made to induce me to make this statement. I presently reside at Cullen, La. I am 26 years old and was born on September 11, 1938, at Plain Dealing, La.

"On June 21, 1964 about 8: 00 P.M., I was having supper at Jimmy Arledge's house, Meridian, Mississippi. Travis Barnette called Arledge on the telephone and told Arledge that the Klan had a job and wanted to know if Arledge and I could go. Arledge asked me if I could go and we went to Akins trailer park on Highway 80 in Meridian, Miss. We did not know what the job was.

"Upon arriving at Akins trailer park we were met by Preacher Killen, Mr. Akins, Jim Jordan and Wayne. I do not know Wayne's last name, but I do know his brother is a police officer in Meridian, Miss. Killen told us that three civil rights workers were in jail in Philadelphia, Miss., and that these three civil rights workers were going to be released from jail and that we were going to catch them and give them a whipping. We were given brown cloth gloves and my car was filled with gas from Mr. Akins gas tank. Jim Snowden, who works for Troy Laundry in Meridian came to Akins trailer park, too. Arledge, Snowden, and Jordan got into my car and we drove to Philadelphia. Killen and Wayne left before we did and we were told that we would meet him there. Killen had a 1962 or 1961 white Buick. When we arrived in Philadelphia, about 9: 30 P.M., we met Killen and he got into my car and directed me where to park and wait for someone to tell us when the three civil rights workers were being released from jail. While we were talking, Killen stated that 'we have a place to bury them, and a man to run the dozer to cover them up.' This was the first time I realized that the three civil rights workers were to be killed. About 5 or 10 minutes after we parked, a patrolman from Philadelphia came to the car and said that 'they are going toward Meridian on Highway 19.' We proceeded out Highway 19 and caught up to a Mississippi State Patrol Car, who pulled into a store on the left hand side of the road. We pulled along side of the patrol car and then another car from Philadelphia pulled in between us. I was driving a 1957 Ford, 4 door, 2 tone blue bearing Louisiana license. The Philadelphia car was a 1958 Chevrolet, 2 door and color maroon. It also had a dent on front right hand fender next to the light. No one got out of the cars, but the driver of the Philadelphia car, who I later learned was named Posey, talked to the patrolmen. Posey then drove away and we followed. About 2 or 3 miles down the Highway Posey's car stopped and pulled off on the right hand side of the road. Posey motioned for me to go ahead. I then drove fast and caught up to the car that the three civil rights workers were in, pulled over to the side of the road and stopped. About a minute or 2 later, Deputy Sheriff Price came along and stopped on the pavement beside my car. Jordan asked him who was going to stop them and Price said that he would and took after them and we followed. The Civil Rights workers turned off Highway 19 on to a side road and drove about a couple of miles before Price stopped them. Price stopped his car behind the 1963 Ford Fairlane Station Wagon driven by the Civil Rights Workers and we stopped behind Price's car. Price was driving a 1956 Chevrolet, 2 door and 2 tone blue in color. Price stated 'I thought you were going back to Meridian if we let you out of jail.' The Civil Rights Workers stated that they were and Price asked them why they were taking the long way around. Price told them to get out and get into his car. They got out of their car and proceed to get into Price's car and then Price took his black-jack and struck Chaney on the back of the head.

"At the junction of Highway 19 and where we turned off, I had let Arledge out of the car to signal the fellows in the Philadelphia car. We then turned around and proceeded back toward Philadelphia. The first car to start back was Price and he had Jim Jordan in the front seat with him and the three civil rights workers in the back seat. I followed next and picked up Arledge at the junction of Highway 19. Snowden drove the 1963 Ford, belonging to the Civil Rights Workers. When we came to Posey's car Price and Snowden pulled over to the left side of the Highway and stopped in front of Posey's car. I stopped behind it. Wayne and Posey and the other men from Philadelphia got into the 1963 Ford and rode with Snowden. I do not know how many men were from Philadelphia. Price then started first and I pulled in behind him and Snowden driving the 1963 Ford came last. I followed Price down Highway 19 and he turned left on to a gravel road. About a mile up the road he stopped and Snowden and I stopped behind him, with about a car length between each car. Before I could get out of the car Wayne ran past my car to Price's car, opened the left rear door, pulled Schwerner out of the car, spun him around so that Schwerner was standing on the left side of the road, with his back to the ditch and said 'Are you that nigger lover' and Schwerner said 'Sir, I know just how you feel.' Wayne had a pistol in his right hand, then shot Schwerner. Wayne then went back to Price's car and got Goodman, took him to the left side of the road with Goodman facing the road, and shot Goodman.

"When Wayne shot Schwerner, Wayne had his hand on Schwerner's shoulder. When Wayne shot Goodman, Wayne was standing within reach of him. Schwerner fell to the left so that he was laying along side the road. Goodman spun around and fell back toward the bank in back.

"At this time Jim Jordan said 'save one for me.' He then got out of Price's car and got Chaney out. I remember Chaney backing up, facing the road, and standing on the bank on the other side of the ditch and Jordan stood in the middle of the road and shot him. I do not remember how many times Jordan shot. Jordan then said. 'You didn't leave me anything but a nigger, but at least I killed me a nigger.' The three civil rights workers were then put into the back of their 1963 Ford wagon. I do not know who put the bodies in the car, but I only put Chaney's foot inside the car, Price then got into his car and drove back toward Highway 19. Wayne, Posey and Jordan then got into the 1963 Ford and started up the road. Snowden, Arledge and another person who I do not know the name of got into my car and we followed. I do not know the roads we took, but went through the outskirts of Philadelphia and to the Dam site on Burrage's property. When we arrived at the Dam site someone said that the bulldozer operator was not there and Wayne, Arledge and I went in my car to find him. We drove out to a paved road and about a mile down the road.

"We saw a 1957 Chevrolet, white and green, parked on the left side of the road. Wayne told me to stop and we backed up to this car. Burrage and 2 other men were in the car. Wayne said that they were already down there and Burrage said to follow them. I followed the 1957 Chevrolet back toward the Dam site, taking a different road, until the Chevrolet stopped. Burrage said 'it is just a little ways over there,' and Wayne and the bulldozer operator walked the rest of the way. The bulldozer operator was about 40 years old, 6 ft - 2 inches tall, slim built and a white male. He was wearing khaki clothes. Arledge and I then followed Burrage and the other man back to Burrage's garage. The other man was a white male, about 40 years old, 5 feet 8 or 9 inches tall, stocky built. Burrage's garage is on the road toward Philadelphia and he had tractors and trailer parked there. His house is across the road.

"We were there about 30 minutes when the other fellows came from the dam site in the 1963 Ford. Burrage got a glass gallon jug and filled it with gasoline to be used to burn the 1963 Ford car owned by the three civil rights workers. Burrage took one of the diesel trucks from under a trailer and said 'I will use this to pick you up, no one will suspect a truck on the road this time at night.' It was then about 1: 00 to 1: 30 in the morning. Snowden, Arledge, Jordan, Wayne and I then got into my car and we drove back toward Philadelphia. When we got to Philadelphia a city patrol car stopped us and we got out. Sheriff Rainey, Deputy Sheriff Price and the City Patrolman, who told us which way the civil rights workers were leaving town, got out of the patrol car. The patrolman was a white male, about 50 years old, 5 feet 8 to 9 inches, 160 lbs., and was wearing a uniform. This was about 2: 00 AM., June 22, 1964. 1 do not know his name, but I have met him before and would know him again.

"We talked for 2 or 3 minutes and then someone said that we better not talk about this and Sheriff Rainey said 'I'll kill anyone who talks, even if it was my own brother.' We then got back into my car and drove back to Meridian and passed Posey's car which was still parked along side the road. We did not stop and there was one or two men standing by Posey's car. We then kept going to Meridian. I took Wayne home, left Jordan and Snowden at Akins Mobile Homes, took Arledge home and went home myself. I have read the above Statement, consisting of this and 9 other pages and they are true and correct to the best of my knowledge and belief. I have signed my initials to the bottom of the first 9 pages and initial mistakes. No force threats or promises were made to induce me to make this statement."

Signed,
Horace Doyle Barnette.

Witnessed:
Henry Rask, Special Agent, FBI Nov. 20, 1964 James A. Wooten, Special Agent, FBI, New Orleans, La. 11-20-64

Appendix III

Appendix III is a sample of some of the literacy tests used to keep black citizens from registering to vote in Mississippi, Louisiana, and Alabama.

SWORN WRITTEN APPLICATION FOR REGISTRATION

[By reason of the provisions of Section 244 of the Constitution of Mississippi and House Bill No. 95, approved March 24, 1955, the applicant for registration, if not physically disabled, is required to fill in this form in his own handwriting in the presence of the registrar and without assistance or suggestion of any other person or memorandum.]

1. WRITE THE DATE OF THIS APPLICATION _____

2. WHAT IS YOUR FULL NAME?_____

3. STATE YOUR AGE AND DATE OF BIRTH _____

4. WHAT IS YOUR OCCUPATION? _____

5. WHERE IS YOUR BUSINESS CARRIED ON? _____

6. BY WHOM ARE YOU EMPLOYED? _____

7. ARE YOU A CITIZEN OF THE UNITED STATES AND AN INHABITANT OF MISSISSIPPI? _____

8. FOR HOW LONG HAVE YOU RESIDED IN MISSISSIPPI? _____

9. WHERE IS YOUR PLACE OF RESIDENCE IN THE DISTRICT? _____

_____

10. SPECIFY THE DATE WHEN SUCH RESIDENCE BEGAN _____

11. STATE YOUR PRIOR PLACE OF RESIDENCE, if any _____

_____

12. CHECK WHICH OATH YOU DESIRE TO TAKE:

    1. General _____   3. Minister's Wife _____

    2. Minister _____   4. If under 21 years at present but 21 years by date of general election _____

13. IF THERE IS MORE THAN ONE PERSON OF YOUR SAME NAME IN THE PRECINCT, BY WHAT NAME DO YOU WISH TO BE CALLED? _____

_____

14. HAVE YOU EVER BEEN CONVICTED OF ANY OF THE FOLLOWING CRIMES: BRIBERY, THEFT, ARSON, OBTAINING MONEY OR GOODS UNDER FALSE PRETENSES, PERJURY, FORGERY, EMBEZZLEMENT OR BIGAMY? _____

15. IF YOUR ANSWER TO QUESTION 14 IS YES, NAME THE CRIME OR CRIMES OF WHICH YOU HAVE BEEN CONVICTED, AND THE DATE AND PLACE OF SUCH CONVICTION OR CONVICTIONS: _____

16. ARE YOU A MINISTER OF THE GOSPEL IN CHARGE OF AN ORGANIZED CHURCH, OR THE WIFE OF SUCH A MINISTER?

17. IF YOUR ANSWER TO QUESTION 16 IS YES, STATE THE LENGTH OF YOUR RESIDENCE IN THE ELECTION DISTRICT _____

18. WRITE AND COPY IN THE SPACE BELOW SECTION _____ OF THE CONSTITUTION OF MISSISSIPPI [Instruction to registrar: You will designate the section of the Constitution and point out same to applicant]:

19. WRITE IN THE SPACE BELOW A REASONABLE INTERPRETATION (THE MEANING)
OF THE SECTION OF THE CONSTITUTION OF MISSISSIPPI WHICH YOU HAVE
JUST COPIED:

20. WRITE IN THE SPACE BELOW A STATEMENT SETTING FORTH YOUR UNDERSTANDING
OF THE DUTIES AND OBLIGATIONS OF CITIZENSHIP UNDER A CONSTITUTIONAL
FORM OF GOVERNMENT:

21. SIGN AND ATTACH HERETO THE OATH OR AFFIRMATION NAMED IN QUESTION 12.:

_____

The applicant will sign his name here

STATE OF MISSISSIPPI   }
COUNTY OF _____ }

　　Sworn to and subscribed before me by the within named
_____ on this, the _____ day of
_____, 19_____.

_____
County Registrar

The State of Louisiana

Literacy Test (This test is to be given to anyone who cannot prove a fifth grade education.)

Do what you are told to do in each statement, nothing more, nothing less. Be careful as one wrong answer denotes failure of the test. You have 10 minutes to complete the test.

1. Draw a line around the number or letter of this sentence.

2. Draw a line under the last word in this line.

3. Cross out the longest word in this line.

4. Draw a line around the shortest word in this line.

5. Circle the first, first letter of the alphabet in this line.

6. In the space below draw three circles, one inside (engulfed by) the other.

7. Above the letter X make a small cross.

8. Draw a line through the letter below that comes earliest in the alphabet.

ZVSBDMKITPHC

9. Draw a line through the two letters below that come last in the alphabet.

ZVBDMKTPHSYC

10. In the first circle below write the last letter of the first word beginning with "L".

11. Cross out the number necessary, when making the number below one million.

10000000000

12. Draw a line from circle 2 to circle 5 that will pass below circle 2 and above circle 4.

13. In the line below cross out each number that is more than 20 but less than 30.

31 16 48 29 53 47 22 37 98 26 20 25

14. Draw a line under the first letter after "h" and draw a line through the second letter after "j".

a b c d e f g h i j k l m n o p q

15. In the space below, write the word "noise" backwards and place a dot over what would be its second letter should it have been written forward.

16. Draw a triangle with a blackened circle that overlaps only its left corner.

17. Look at the line of numbers below, and place on the blank, the number that should come next.

2 4 8 16 ____

18. Look at the line of numbers below, and place on the blank, the number that should come next.

3   6   9   ____   15

19. Draw in the space below, a square with a triangle in it, and within that same triangle draw a circle with a black dot in it.

20. Spell backwards, forwards.

21. Print the word vote upside down, but in the correct order.

22. Place a cross over the tenth letter in this line, a line under the first space in this sentence, and circle around the last the in the second line of this sentence.

23. Draw a figure that is square in shape. Divide it in half by drawing a straight line from its northeast corner to its southwest corner, and then divide it once more by drawing a broken line from the middle of its western side to the middle of its eastern side.

24. Print a word that looks the same whether it is printed frontwards or backwards.

25. Write down on the line provided, what you read in the triangle below:

Paris
in the
the spring

26. In the third square below, write the second letter of the fourth word.

27. Write right from the left to the right as you see it spelled here.

28. Divide a vertical line in two equal parts by bisecting it with a curved horizontal line that is only straight at its spot bisection of the vertical.

29. Write every other word in this first line and print every third word in same line, (original type smaller and first line ended at comma) but capitalize the fifth word that you write.

30. Draw five circles that one common inter-locking part.

Alabama Literacy Test

1. Which of the following is a right guaranteed by the Bill of Rights?
   _____ Public Education
   _____ Employment
   _____ Trial by Jury
   _____ Voting

2. The federal census of population is taken every five years.
   _____ True _____ False

3. If a person is indicted for a crime, name two rights which he has.

   _____

   _____

4. A U.S. senator elected at the general election in November takes office the following year on what date?

   _____

5. A President elected at the general election in November takes office the following year on what date?

   _____

6. Which definition applies to the word "amendment?"
   _____ Proposed change, as in a Constitution
   _____ Make of peace between nationals at war
   _____ A part of the government

7. A person appointed to the U.S. Supreme Court is appointed for a term of _____.

8. When the Constitution was approved by the original colonies, how many states had to ratify it in order for it to be in effect?

   _____

9. Does enumeration affect the income tax levied on citizens in various states? _____

10. A person opposed to swearing in an oath may say, instead:
I (solemnly)

_____

11. To serve as President of the United States, a person must have attained:
_____ 25 years of age
_____ 35 years of age
_____ 40 years of age
_____ 45 years of age

12. What words are required by law to be on all coins and paper currency of the U.S.?

_____

_____

13. The Supreme Court is the chief lawmaking body of the state.
_____ True _____ False

14. If a law passed by a state is contrary to provisions of the U.S. Constitution, which law prevails?

_____

_____

15. If a vacancy occurs in the U.S. Senate, the state must hold an election, but meanwhile the place may be filled by a temporary appointment made by

_____

_____.

16. A U.S. senator is elected for a term of _____ years.

17. Appropriation of money for the armed services can be only for a period limited to _____ years.

18. The chief executive and the administrative offices make up the _____ branch of government.

19. Who passes laws dealing with piracy?

   _____

   _____

20. The number of representatives which a state is entitled to have in the House of Representatives is based on

   _____

21. The Constitution protects an individual against punishments which are _____ and _____.

22. When a jury has heard and rendered a verdict in a case, and the judgment on the verdict has become final, the defendant cannot again be brought to trial for the same cause.

   _____ True _____ False

23. Name two levels of government which can levy taxes:

   _____

   _____

24. Communism is the type of government in:

   _____ U.S.

   _____ Russia

   _____ England

25. Cases tried before a court of law are two types, civil and

   _____.

26. By a majority vote of the members of Congress, the Congress can change provisions of the Constitution of the U.S.

   _____ True _____ False

27. For security, each state has a right to form a

   _____.

28. The electoral vote for President is counted in the presence of two bodies. Name them:

   _____

   _____

29. If no candidate for President receives a majority of the electoral vote, who decides who will become President?

_____

30. Of the original 13 states, the one with the largest representation in the first Congress was

_____.

31. Of which branch of government is the Speaker of the House a part?
_____ Executive
_____ Legislative
_____ Judicial

32. Capital punishment is the giving of a death sentence.
_____ True _____ False

33. In case the President is unable to perform the duties of his office, who assumes them?

_____

_____

34. "Involuntary servitude" is permitted in the U.S. upon conviction of a crime.
_____ True _____ False

35. If a state is a party to a case, the Constitution provides that original jurisdiction shall be in

_____.

36. Congress passes laws regulating cases which are included in those over which the U.S. Supreme Court has

_____ jurisdiction.

37. Which of the following is a right guaranteed by the Bill of Rights of the U.S. Constitution.
_____ Public Housing
_____ Education
_____ Voting
_____ Trial by Jury

38. The Legislatures of the states decide how presidential electors may be chosen.

 _____ True _____ False

39. If it were proposed to join Alabama and Mississippi to form one state, what groups would have to vote approval in order for this to be done?

 _____

 _____

40. The Vice President presides over

 _____.

41. The Constitution limits the size of the District of Columbia to

 _____.

42. The only laws which can be passed to apply to an area in a federal arsenal are those passed by _____ provided consent for the purchase of the land is given by the

 _____.

43. In which document or writing is the "Bill of Rights" found?

 _____.

44. Of which branch of government is a Supreme Court justice a part?

 _____ Executive

 _____ Legislative

 _____ Judicial

45. If no person receives a majority of the electoral votes, the Vice President is chosen by the Senate.

 _____ True _____ False

46. Name two things which the states are forbidden to do by the U.S. Constitution. _____

 _____ _____

 _____

47. If election of the President becomes the duty of the U.S. House of Representatives and it fails to act, who becomes President and when? _____

_____

48. How many votes must a person receive in order to become President if the election is decided by the U.S. House of Representatives? _____

49. How many states were required to approve the original Constitution in order for it to be in effect?

_____

50. Check the offenses which, if you are convicted of them, disqualify you for voting:
_____ Murder
_____ Issuing worthless checks
_____ Petty larceny
_____ Manufacturing whiskey

51. The Congress decides in what manner states elect presidential electors.
_____ True _____ False

52. Name two of the purposes of the U.S. Constitution.

_____

_____

53. Congress is composed of

_____.

54. All legislative powers granted in the U.S. Constitution may legally be used only by _____

_____.

55. The population census is required to be made very _____ years.

56. Impeachments of U.S. officials are tried by

_____.

57. If an effort to impeach the President of the U.S. is made, who presides at the trial? _____

_____

58. On the impeachment of the chief justice of the Supreme Court of the U.S., who tries the case? _____

_____

59. Money is coined by order of:
    _____ U.S. Congress
    _____ The President's Cabinet
    _____ State Legislatures

60. Persons elected to cast a state's vote for U.S. President and Vice President are called presidential _____

_____.

61. Name one power which is exclusively legislative and is mentioned in one of the parts of the U.S. Constitution above

_____.

62. If a person flees from justice into another state, who has authority to ask for his return? _____

_____

63. Whose duty is it to keep Congress informed of the state of the union? _____

64. If the two houses of Congress cannot agree on adjournment, who sets the time?

_____

65. When presidential electors meet to cast ballots for President, must all electors in a state vote for the same person for President or can they vote for different persons if they so choose?

_____

_____

66. After the presidential electors have voted, to whom do they send the count of their votes? _____

_____

67. The power to declare war is vested in

_____.

68. Any power and rights not given to the U.S. or prohibited to the states by the U.S. Constitution are specified as belonging to whom? _____

Appendix IV

This document was written by the Council of Federated Organizations (COFO) in 1964 to give guidance to local civil rights workers to help organize the Mississippi Freedom Democratic Party to give black citizens a political voice in state and national elections.

CHALLENGE OF THE MISSISSIPPI FREEDOM DEMOCRATIC PARTY

I. DEVELOPMENT OF THE MISSISSIPPI FREEDOM DEMOCRATIC P ARTY

Three basic considerations underlie the development of the Mississippi Freedom Democratic Party and its plans to challenge the seating of the delegation of the Mississippi Democratic Party at the 1964 Democratic National Convention. They are:

1. The long history of systematic and studied exclusion of Negro citizens from equal participation in the political processes of the state grows more flagrant and intensified daily .

2. The Mississippi Democratic Party has conclusively demonstrated its lack of loyalty to the National Democratic Party, in the past , and currently indicates no intent ion of supporting the platform of the 1964 Democratic Convention.

3. The intransigent and fanatical determination of the State's political power-structure to maintain status-quo, clearly demonstrates that the "Mississippi closed society," as Professor James W. Silver of the University of Mississippi asserts, is without leadership or moral resources to reform itself, and hence can only be brought into the mainstream of the twentieth century by forces outside of itself.

A. PARTY DISCRIMINATION:

The Mississippi Democratic Party controls the legislative, executive and judicial branches of the government of the State. All 49 senators. and all but one of 122 representatives are Democrat s. Repeatedly , the State legislature has passed laws and established regulations designed to discriminate against prospective Negro voters. The 1963 gubernatorial campaign was largely directed towards restricting the Negro vote. The state convention is being held in the Jackson Municipal Auditorium and the Heidelburg Hotel, both of which are segregated. In its devotion to racism and suppression and oppression of minority expression, the Mississippi Democratic Party prevents Negro Democrats and white persons who disagree with the partyt's racist stance from participating in party programs and decisions.

B. PARTY DISLOYALTY:

Mississippi citizens who desire t o do so cannot support the National Democratic goals by joining the Mississippi Democratic Party. The Mississippi Democratic Party has declared in public speeches and printed matter that it is NOT a part of the National Democratic Party. The campaign literature for the election of Governor Paul B. Johnson, in 1963, is a case in point, as the following excerpts show: ••• "Our Mississippi Democratic Party is entirely independent and free of the influence of domination of any national party" ••••• "The Mississippi Democratic Party which long ago separated itself from the National Democratic Party, and which has fought consistently everything both national parties stand for •••••••"

In 1960 the Mississippi Democratic Party failed to honor its pledge to support the nominees of the Democratic National Convention. Immediately after the convention the Mississippi party convened a convention and voted to support unpledged electors in an effort to defeat the nominees of the Democratic National Convention.

C. THE CLOSED SOCIETY:

"It can be argued that in the history of the United States democracy has produced great leaders in great crises. Sad as it may be. the opposite has been true in Mississippi. As yet there is little evidence that the society of the closed mind will ever possess the moral resources to reform itself, or the capacity for self-examination, or even the tolerance of self-examination."

—from "Mississippi: The Closed Society," COFO position paper by James W. Silver

Civil rights groups working in Mississippi are convinced that political and social justice can not be won in Mississippi without massive interest and support of the country as a whole, backed by the authority of the federal government . As the political leadership of

Mississippi feel threatened by the winds of change, they devise new and more extensive legal weapons and police powers. Police preparations are now being made to harass, intimidate and threaten the educational and registration program scheduled to be conducted in Mississippi this summer. Five new bills. prohibiting picketing, banning the distribution of boycott literature, restricting the movement of groups, establishing curfews, authorizing municipalities to pool police manpower and equipment, and increasing penalties that may be assessed by city courts — have been hurriedly signed into law. Other similar bills are still pending.

I I. ORGANIZATIONAL STRUCTURE OF THE FREEDOM DEMOCRATIC PARTY

To give Negro citizens of Mississippi an experience in political democracy and to establish a channel through which all citizens, Negro and white, can actively support the principles and programs of the National Democratic Party, the Mississippi Freedom Democratic Party was conceived. The Council of Federated Organizations (COFO), a confederation of all the national and local civil rights and citizenship education groups in Mississippi is assisting local citizens to develop the Mississippi Freedom Democratic Party. This party is open to all citizens regardless of race. It was officially established at a meeting in Jackson, Mississippi on April 26th; and the approximately 200 dele- gates present elected a temporary state executive committee, which will be responsible for setting precinct and other state meetings. These meetings will parallel those of the Mississippi Democratic Party, and every effort will be made to comply with all state laws which apply to the formation of political parties. Registered voters in the Freedom Democratic Party will attempt to attend precinct and county meetings of the Mississippi Democratic Party.

The Mississippi Freedom Democratic Parry is presently engaged in three major efforts:

(1) Freedom Registration; (2) Freedom Candidates; and (3) Convention Challenge .

1. FREEDOM REGISTRA TION:

Official registration figures show that only some 20,000 Negroes are registered in Mississippi as compared to 500,000 whites. This represents less than 7% of the 435,000 Negroes 21 years of age in the state. The Freedom Registration is designed to show that thousands of Negroes want to become registered voters . By se~ting up registrars and deputy registrars in each of the 82 counties of the state9 300,000 persons may be registered in the Freedom Registration. Last November some 83,000 Negroes were registered in a mock gubernatorial race. In the present drive, 75,000 are reported registered , and this will be greatly stepped up when the summer program officially begins at the end of June. This registration will use simplified registration forms based on voting applications used in several northern States. Any person who registers in the Freedom Registration will be eligible to vote in the Freedom Democratic Party Convention and participate in party work.

2. FREEDOM CANDIDA TES:

The four (4) candidates who qualified to run in the June 2 primary in Mississippi were nominees of the Freedom Democratic Party and in addition to their bid in the regular Democratic primary, they will also run in a mock election under the Mississippi Freedom Democratic Party in November. This will help to establish the fact that thousands of Negroes are deprived of citizenship participation because of the racist character of Mississippi's voter registration procedures.

The four candidates are:

Mrs. Victoria Gray, opposing Senator John Stennls,

Mrs. Fannie Lou Hamer, opposing Representative Jamie L. Whiten;

The Reverend John Cameron, opposing Representative William M. Colmer;

Mr. James Houston . opposing Representative John Bell Williams.

The platforms of the candidates of the Freedom Democratic Party articulate the needs of all the people of Mississippi, such as

— anti-poverty programs, Medicare, aid to education, rural development, urban renewal , and the guarantee of constitutional rights to all. This is in sharp contrast to the lack of real issues in the campaigns of the candidates who won in the primary Senator Stennis did not even bother to campaign in the state.

3. THE CHALLENGE TO THE DEMOCRATIC NATIONAL CONVENTION:

Delegates from the Freedom Democratic Party will challenge the seating of the "old-line" Mississippi delegation at the Democratic National Convention this August in Atlantic CitYl, New Jersey. These delegates will have been chosen through precinct meetings, county conventions, caucuses in congressional districts, and at a state-wide convention of the Freedom Democratic Party. The State Executive Committee will be ratified and the national committeeman and committeewoman will be chosen at this state-wide convention.

All steps necessary to preparing and formally presenting the challenge of the Freedom Democratic Party are being taken.

BUT WE NEED YOUR COOPERATION AND HELP!

*** We need convention delegates to champion the cause of representative government in Mississippi

*** We need people who will speak out in the credentials committee and on the convention floor

*** We need hundreds of Democrats — individuals and organizations — to instruct their delegates, petition their representatives, party leaders and the President to face up to the fact that only a renegade democratic party exists in Mississippi which enjoys the benefits of national affiliation but spurns all responsibilities and can only continue to bring disgrace to the National Democratic Party.

MISSISSIPPI FREEDOM DEMOCRATIC PARTY
Convention Headquarters Gem Hotel
505 Pacific Avenue Atlantic City, New Jersey
Tel.-344-7129
1017 Lynch Street
Jackson, Mississippi 39203
Tel.-Area Code 601-352-9605

Appendix V

This document is a handout used to educate black citizens engaged in agriculture to vote in the U.S. Department of Agriculture Agricultural Stabilization and Conservation Service elections.

ASCS ELECTIONS

VOTE DECEMBER 2nd

ASCS MEANS -

AGRICULTURAL STABILIZATION

CONSERVATION SERVICE

Last year Negroes were on the ballot for the ASCS committee for the first time in Mississippi. Negroes ran in 12 counties. SOME WON. They won in spite of the trouble from the white people and some ASCS employees.

The elections in Mississippi will be December 2nd this year. Here is some information about the ASCS and the elections.

ELECTION DAY

ABOUT THE ASCS

In the 1930's farmers were in a bad way like today, farmers didn't get much money for their crops, but they had to pay a lot for the things they bought from the stores. Because farmers were organizing and protesting the Federal Government tried to do something to help small farmers.

They Set Up Four Programs:

First - PRICE SUPPORTS

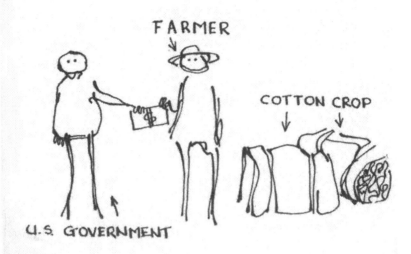

These made sure that farmers would be able to sell their crops at something near a decent price. The government buys enough of certain crops (like cotton, corn, tobacco and peanuts) to keep the price up.

Second - ACREAGE CONTROLS

Like white cotton farmers are not allowed to plant too much of certain crops. This way farmers would not produce too much. This means that what was raised would get a decent price.

-4-

Third - ACREAGE CONVERSION

People would be hurt if they could not plant all their land because of crop controls. So farmers can get loans and money to plant their land and money to plant their land in trees, grass, or certain crops.

Fourth -   COMMODITY CREDIT
CORPORATION (CCC)

Prices usually fall at harvest time, so the government set up a loan program. After harvest farmers can store their crops and borrow money from the CCC.

Then they can sell their crops when the price is better.

These programs are still being used today. They are all

run through one office, the ASCS office. ASCS stands for

Agricultural Stabilization and Conservation Service. Each

county has an ASCS office at the county seat.

ASCS COMMITTEES

When the government set the ASCS up it tried to make sure that all farmers would have a say in how the ASCS was run. This is how they did that:

FOR AN EXAMPLE

TAKE

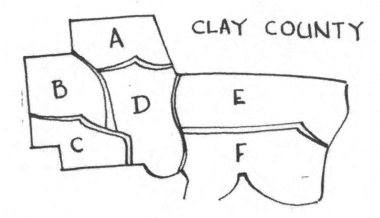

CLAY COUNTY

1. Each county is divided into communities. The farmers in each community elect three (3) men to the community committee once a year. Anyone who farms can vote: tenants, sharecroppers, landowners, and wives who actively work on the farm.

-7-

2. Each county has a 3-man committee. It is elected by the community committmen.

THREE-MAN COMMITTEE

This committee
    a. gives out cotton allottments

    b. decides who gets extra acreage

    c. hires the measurers

    d. decides who gets CCC loans

    e. hires the office supervisor

3. There is a State Director. In Mississippi he is Mr. Sullivan. He can handle complaints.

He is supposed to pass information on the committee.

He is appointed by the Secretary of Agriculture in Washington, D. C.

— — —

4. There is a National Director. His name is Raymond Fitzgerald. His office is in Washington, D. C.

— — —

5. The Secretary of Agriculture Orville Freeman, is over him. He is appointed by the congress of the United States.

ASCS Elections

ASCS ELECTIONS

The elections for the community committee will be December 2nd. This is how the election works.

By November 2nd, All farmers, tenants, sharecroppers, owners, and their wives who actively work on the farm should get a letter from the ASCS office.

MAKE SURE
YOUR NAME
iS ON THE
A.S.C.S. Book!

If you do not receive a letter and a ballot by the 2nd of November you should go to the ASCS office. If you and your wife own the land you work you should take a copy of the deed showing the names of the owners. Sharecroppers and tenants can take a statement to the ASCS office written by the owner of the land they work on. A receipt for a purchase of fertilizer, seed, farm machinery, etc. can be taken to the ASCS office. The receipt is to show that you have an interest in the crop.

Wives of land owners, sharecroppers, and tenants can vote if they can show that they have an interest in the crop. Their name should be on the deed, statement, or receipt.

-10-

POINTS TO REMEMBER

1. YOU DO NOT HAVE TO BE A REGISTERED VOTER
2. YOU DO NOT HAVE TO OWN THE LAND YOU LIVE ON
3. YOU DO NOT HAVE TO BE ABLE TO READ AND WRITE

HERE'S HOW
TO
MAIL
YOUR
BALLOT

When you get your ballot there will be 2 envelopes. One will be a plain envelope and the other will have a statement printed on the back. You should mark your ballot and seal printed on the back. You should mark your ballot and put it inside the plain envelope and seal it. Then put the sealed plain envelope inside the envelope with the statement on the back. The statement says that the ballot was marked by you personally. If you can not sign your name you can make your sign and have a witness sign the ballot.

-11-

After this letter comes out, any eligible voter (anyone who farms) can be nominated and his name put on the ballot.

To nominate someone for the community committee election, six (6) or more eligible voters who live in the same community sign a petition. The petition can say something like: "We nominate Clyde Doe for the ASCS community committee."

Communities in Clay County

SEE MAP ON PAGE 7

Brand and Happy Hollow are in community A
on the map, Pheba and Cedar Bluff are in C,
and so on.

A - Brand, Happy Hollow

B - Montpelier, Pine Bluff, Palestine, Cairo

C- Pheba, Cedar Bluff

D - Abbott, Moon Valley

E - White's Station

F - Tibbee, Waverly

The person who is nominated must live in the same
community as the people who sign his petition. He must be
able to vote in the ASCS election. The letter you get should
tell you what community you live in.

After the petition is filled out, it should be taken to the
ASCS office. It must be in by November 12th. It is a good
idea to take it in several days earlier. That way if there
are any mistakes on the petition, they can be corrected.

On NOVEMBER 22nd the ASCS

office will mail out the ballots.

They must be mailed back by

DECEMBER 2nd!

–14–

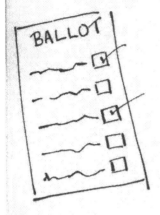

YOU CAN

VOTE FOR

1

2

3

or 5

PEOPLE

You DO NOT have to vote for ALL 5

On Election Day -

the ballots will be counted at the ASUS office

EVERYONE WHO VOTED

CAN GO

and

WATCH

-16-

The three (3) men and women in each community who get the most votes are the community committemen. The next two are alternates. They will serve if one of the regular members is absent.

Not long after the election all the community committee-men will meet and elect 3 men to the county committee and 2 alternates.

If people we choose are to get on the

County Committee,   we must win more

than half of the seats on the community committee

-18-

TELL YOUR FRIENDS ABOUT THE ELECTION

About the Author

Charles O. Prickett was born in Carbondale, Illinois. He attended Southern Illinois University and the University of Illinois for his undergraduate degree in philosophy and math. He earned a Master's Degree from the University of  Illinois, attended Syracuse University, earned a J.D. Degree from the University of New Hampshire (Franklin Pierce Law Center), and a Ph.D. from the University of Arizona.

Charles has worked many different jobs, from carpenter and plumber and mechanic, to professor and public school teacher. He is currently an attorney in Santa Rosa, California and has been a pro tem judge in small claims and traffic court for over thirty years.

Additional copies of this book may be ordered at:
www.createspace/5094129

Made in the USA
San Bernardino, CA
06 October 2015